Intimidation by Political Correctness

A Distinctively Democrat Phenomenon

J.W. Brasher

authorHOUSE®

AuthorHouse™
1663 Liberty Drive
Bloomington, IN 47403
www.authorhouse.com
Phone: 1-800-839-8640

First published by AuthorHouse   4/25/2011

ISBN: 978-1-4520-7006-3 (sc)
ISBN: 978-1-4520-7007-0 (hc)
ISBN: 978-1-4520-7008-7 (e)

Library of Congress Control Number: 2010913187

Printed in the United States of America

This book is printed on acid-free paper.

J.W. BRASHER
BORN
2 DECEMBER 1931
TO THE
LATE GREAT
UNITED STATES OF AMERICA

CONTENTS

PART II

PART III

FOREWORD

To avoid repeated disclaimers (this is not necessary for Republicans or Independents) throughout this little book, where I lump a total of anything or anyone into a mold, please note that I acknowledge the exception or two or three to everything. For example, should I say that everyone on this planet is subject to gravity; I know man can create circumstances that yield zero gravity for finite periods of time or conditions. One could call this profiling. Should I state that the ACLU is a democrat, liberal, radical organization intent not on what the name would lead one to believe, but rather on harming the government and judicial system that made this country great. There is possibly, but not probably, an exception to the ACLU also.

Up front once again, let it be said that throughout this little book, one may find opinions expressed. This is contrary to the television media; radio, in particular National Public Radio; and most newspaper editors and columnists, where no such warning is given. Instead, their presentations are presented as gospel. Nor is there an "other side" given by the media (except for, of course, Fox News). Few hard figures have been given for the reader to fret over. Instead, I chose to use non-specifics; e.g., "most," or "high percentage," et cetera. For readers wishing to comment or question any position, I will not be drawn into a battle of a few percentage points, unless it would tip the scales above or below 50 percent. In that case, presented with objective evidence, I will graciously accept a correction without asking the definition of "a," "is," or "what."

PART I

GLORY YEARS FOR THE REPUBLIC

I consider the high-water mark of the American Republic to be the years 1940 through 1960, a plateau to be the years 1960 through 1963, and a decline from 1964 to present. For most of the declining years, it has been an arithmetic decline, but starting in the early 1990s, the decline became nearly logarithmic. At the Republic's high-water mark, it was solvent, a benefactor of the world, secure and confident of its future. These were glory years for the country and most of its citizens. These were truly days of wine and roses.

Although all radicals and many liberals despise scientists and their efforts, it is the only sector of our society that has progressed for the better in the past five to five and a half decades. Sure there have been missteps, mostly, in my opinion, due to human error. Concrete progress in all scientific and technology areas, from medicine, to automobiles, to communication, to information processing, to housing, to food, to the environment, can be seen all around.

Not so in our social/civic/personal/government/legal/education institutions. In fact, every one of these endeavors, where the human element is the only or the predominant player, has deteriorated to disaster proportions. Advances in the sciences and in technology are the product of analytical thinking and reason, two items in short supply in a liberal. Take our public school systems. From Chicago to New Orleans to Los Angeles to New York, our public education systems are disaster areas. Certainly they are no match for the schools prior to 1960, when our education system was the envy of the world.

Even with tossing out the old IQ test as "not relevant" and the successive watering down of replacement examinations, the educators still can't get the students to perform. Some colleges do not require a SAT, and there is even talk of doing away with the SAT altogether. This thinking has exacerbated the weak links of what was once a great educational system, plunging it into failure. Do I feel bad for the adults that have facilitated this failure? Not on your life... It's the children and the country that I feel sorry for.

Even with teaching the test and lax test environments, lowered passing grade, et cetera, et cetera, test scores continue to fall. The students would be far, far better off if they took twice as long, and schools just kept them in first grade until they learned the material. Self-esteem is acquired by learning, not by being passed on unprepared.

Finally, I believe nothing put out by the educators. Over the years they have proven themselves untrustworthy. In a recent period of about ten days, my locally distributed newspapers reported that grades had improved, slightly. A few days later, the papers reported that national test scores were down—again.

To highlight another failure, one only has to consider what has happened to the judicial system. Any resulting justice in a courtroom today is purely accidental. Today the "judicial branch of the government" is actually only a hollow system. There was a day when I would have trusted my life to a jury of twelve peers. Today, I would trust nothing to a jury. Think about it for a minute. In the courtroom a witness swears to "tell the truth, the whole truth, and nothing but the truth." Not so for judges or lawyers. A lawyer can lie in court. Think of the significance of that. And, of course, they do lie, they mislead, and they manipulate. It is hardly necessary to note that with a few exceptions, all judges are lawyers.

Recently there was an obituary in the newspaper that printed a picture of an aged lady, as well as a picture of her when she was perhaps twenty-five or thirty years old. She was born in 1921, and age had taken a heavy toll on her outward appearance. In the younger photo, she was a beautiful woman in full bloom. An analogy is there with this country. At the time of that younger photo (1940–1951), this country was in full flower: respected by the world, wealthy, almost unlimited industrial capacity, the best vehicles (and best looking) in the world, a united population, stable energy prices. The price of a gallon of gasoline could go for years with only a few cents worth of change, and this was sometimes due to a local "gas war." Millions from the world over wanted to come to the U.S. Of course, millions still do, but in those days it was to seek opportunity. Today it is to get on the welfare gravy train.

We were a civilized and safe society then. There were hardly any streets in the entire country where one would have felt unsafe alone at night. This was certainly true when I was a student at Central High School. Anywhere in the city anytime; it was no problem. In that day, it was not unusual to leave the family home and the family car unlocked. Sometimes the keys were even left in the family vehicle. More than once in college, I took my girlfriend downtown to the movies (when there was still a downtown) and left the top down on my car while we were at the movie, no problem. Contrast that with the ugliness and evils of today's situation in any and all areas.

Of the many issues facing our country today one of the more troubling is the issue of public and personal safety. In this country today, you are not safe anywhere or anytime. Not in your home, not in your car, not in the heart of town, not at the local fast-food shop, not at school, not at work, not in church, not in the hospital, not in the grocery-store parking lot, not on the interstate, not in the courtroom, not in the park, not on a military base, not even stopping at a local convenience store to ask directions to the football stadium. This past fall a man and his wife drove in from out of town to see their grandson play football. When they stopped to ask for directions, the man was shot in the head and killed during an attempted robbery, with his terrified wife on the car seat beside him. These criminals today are so bold, so aggressive, so stupid, and so confident of either not getting caught or beating the rap, the mall parking lot at high noon is fine with them. Would you like to know why this man was shot dead? The male who shot him wanted money to go to the fair.

At this point it must be noted that the males involved in this killing were all minorities. The paper distributed in this area contained an article today about the trial of one of the suspects. The paper reported that as the widow of the slain man entered the courtroom, she encountered insults from the friends and family of the minority male on trial. The article reported that one man addressed the widow with a "screw you," and a woman said, "This court's a [expletive deleted] joke." Now this is in the courtroom, and if anyone did anything to address that awful conduct, the paper did not report it. In a civilized society, one would have expected those people to show some sympathy or remorse for this tragedy, but not these people. I would describe their comments as "hate speech," if there were ever any validity to that term. No one arrested them for their crude and insulting behavior. Recall this conduct and these words when you read the pieces on simple "politically correct" speech, and compare the consequences of "politically correct" with hate/ crude/insulting speech in a courtroom. It is totally dependent on whether or not one is a "protected" species. No mass media outcry here. According to a later article, this crowd got so rowdy during the trial, the judge had to threaten to clear the courtroom.

VICTIMS' RIGHTS

This little section may not sit well with those legal people that operate in the criminal activities world. It is believable that a lawyer representing a criminal would want to stand up for a criminals' "rights" and within reason that is acceptable. Going to the extent of getting a guilty person off, however, is irrational and defeats justice.

In any discussion of the rights of a victim versus the rights of the criminal, contrary to the legal arena I give the victim the benefit of the doubt, not the criminal. The victim has many rights, all of which override any criminal activity. First the victim has a right to his person, his family, his spouse, his property, his home, his business and his privacy. He has the right to undisturbed life, liberty and the pursuit of happiness from any criminal activity. Violation of any of these by a criminal trumps the criminal for he is conducting illegal activities as he violates the victims' rights. The victim has a right not to have to suffer injury or death, not to have to be absent from his work or pleasures, not to have to appear in court, not to suffer injury or death of a loved one, not to have to endure emotional distress and not to have to undergo a hundred other things required of him as the result of the irresponsibility of a criminal. He has the right to expect the laws, the police and the courts to provide an encumbering environment to the criminal such that the individual citizen expects no violations of his rights by the criminal. Today these are in massive failure. He has a right to expect the combination of these three to say, in effect: "Don't worry; I've got your back." Whatever it takes; profiling, tossing out an outdated court system and starting all over again, the masses of American citizens are due that under the constitution.

In addressing this subject I recognize the difficulty in identifying the victim or the criminal in some bar room brawls. Not to dismiss these of no concern my point is to address the more typical situation - that of a guy sitting by the fireside in his own home or walking down the street minding in his own business when he is violently robbed or assaulted. In the totality of it, it is the criminal that is the bully, the aggressor, the violator of the law, the creator of tragedy, the killer of joy, all of these and more. I am outraged at the criminal and that the legal system seems to handle him with kid gloves. As for me, I stand with the victim and in some cases that is the public. I can readily make a distinction between tainted evidence and a tainted method of obtaining evidence. Valid evidence necessary to secure justice for the victim and/or the criminal must be admissible evidence else justice may be compromised or denied. That the courts have allowed valid evidence to be excluded from a trial only convinces me more that the courts desperately need some adult supervision. Tainted methods is another subject entirely, however tainted evidence is expected to be tossed out for it can generally result in unfair treatment of one of the parties.

A democrat would never understand my dad. My dad died in the mid 1950s of a heart attack at the now young age of fifty-seven. He was a college graduate, class of 1923. He never owned an air-conditioned house or car. Both of these innovations were in their infancy at that time of his death. Still, could he be here today, he would rapidly understand the scientific and technological advances of the past fifty-three years. However, he would never understand the people and the society we have become. Frankly, his son is here today, and he doesn't understand it.

REAL POVERTY

In recent years the government has made a big deal out of "poor" people (read, "potential vote"), a war on poverty, arbitrary poverty levels assigned by the government, subsidized housing, medical care, food stamps (now called an EBT card and looks like a credit card), Social Security for people who never paid into system, aid to dependent children, subsidized housing, subsidized utilities, day care, free transportation, preferential job and school treatment, et cetera. Probably no one really knows how many programs there are out there created solely to help the so-called poor and minorities. For the total, one must count the numerous non-government "charity" organizations also. Has it done any good? It most certainly has, no question about it. Now they can drive to the grocery store to use their EBT cards in nice-looking air-conditioned vehicle, with multiple rings on their fingers and dressed as well or better than the cash customers. In fact, most of the people that support those giveaway programs have never seen real poverty eyeball to eyeball. Allow me to relate a short story that will paint a vivid picture of honest, hard-core poverty.

In 1940 my dad, who was with the Corps of Engineers, was sent out west to survey for a dam and airfield runway extensions. Although we had been in a new home for less than a year in the east-central part of Mississippi, we moved into my great-grandfather's house on the property next to my grandparents. The property was located about three miles outside a small town in rural Mississippi. Of course, in those days the entire state was only a stone's throw from rural. So we spent the school year there while Dad was on his assignment in Texas, Kansas, and Oklahoma.

The event that I shall always remember, and that I cannot tell without shedding a tear even today, took place as I recall in January 1941, when I was one month into my ninth year. It was a bitterly cold, overcast day. My grandfather had two tenant houses on the property; one down the hill near the creek, and one in a field behind the house. At that time, the second house had a family of five living in it—a man, his wife, and three children. The oldest boy was my age.

In those days help to the poor, and these people were poor, consisted of "commodities," which I believe they could draw once per month. Commodities consisted of cheese, fatback, powdered milk, butter, and not much else. One could use fatback to cook with, and to make lard and pork rinds. This stuff had to be picked up in the nearest town, which was about three miles away. Now my grandfather had a fairly new black two-door 1940 Pontiac. No radio, just plain dependable transportation. I'm sure the man of the tenant family never thought to ask my grandfather to give them a ride into town, and I did not see them when they came around the house on their walk into town. But on their return, I saw them as they topped the hill in front of the house and headed toward the tenant house to the rear. I was standing in my grandmother's front room with a roaring fire in the fireplace. As I looked out the front window to the road, I saw it had begun to sleet lightly. Little puddles were collecting in low spots on the front lawn. What struck me and will always live with me was that as the family walked by carrying their few commodities, I noticed the little boy my age. He was <u>barefoot.</u> That, people, is poverty, and it did not need a government agency to define it. It spoke for itself.

Now before you liberals get your drawers wrapped around your outrage, permit me to point out that these tenants were white people. I never knew my grandfather to have anything but white sharecroppers.

RIGHTS VERSUS RESPONSIBILITIES

The following is a true story not known to everyone because the democrat or media would never pass it on. At one time Gandhi was approached by the author of a new book with a request that Gandhi endorse it in some way. The name of the book, as I recall, was *The Rights of Man*. Gandhi refused his request, correctly observing that there is no way one can write of the rights of man without concurrently writing of the responsibilities or duties of man. Now a democrat is fully informed on the former and totally ignorant of the latter; and this lacking accounts in large part for the democrats' many failings.

POLITICAL CORRECTNESS

Contributing to the national decline not in an insignificant way is political correctness. Although PC is a relatively recent negative factor, it is nevertheless a dangerous practice. Under this code a person cannot call a pig a pig, he cannot tell his favorite Polish joke, he cannot joke about a foreign "religion," but he can of course joke about Christianity or Christians. In short, he is denied freedom of speech. He is denied his free speech not because he is necessarily afraid of offending someone, but because he may be slapped with a federal charge or fired from his job or assaulted. PC comes about because some segments of our population do not want to hear comments about themselves, their conduct, manners, appearance, or dress. Generally, the media support their position, and an off ender is crucified, fired, demoted, or whatever as punishment. This is not about someone lying, or the truth, or at least someone's opinion of the truth. Thus, in the end a person is denied his freedom of speech, because some segment of the population doesn't want to hear it—and is supported by the media. In fact, the media make political correctness possible. For without the big mouth of the media, the off ending word or event would vanish like fog in a hot sun.

The scope of political correctness is not limited to speech. It extends to conduct, appearance, and even business. And it is so powerful that businesses that have for years capitalized on the Christmas trade now boycott Christmas. This does not come about for no reason. It happens because not every customer is a Christian, and recognizing Christmas could perhaps offend someone. Now the store is still looking to benefit from all those Christian dollars that do come in. They are not about to reject those. What I object to is not so much that companies refuses to recognize Christmas, as their reason for the action. They caved in to blackmail in the form of political correctness. A governor in one state put up a Christmas tree in the governor's mansion, only it was not a Christmas tree. He called it a holiday tree. Actually it was a case of intimidation by political correctness. People, you need to be aware of the vastness of political correctness and its negative impact on our country.

Political correctness is an invention of the latter part of the twentieth century. It was and is an evil and oppressive invention. Political correctness is intended to deny freedom of speech, to intimidate, and to punish offenders. Political correctness is not a law enacted by Congress. It is not the result of a Supreme Court decision (although the courts are clearly sympathetic to its practice and purposes).

Political correctness is almost exclusively a baby birthed by the mass media (television) in support of some cause, person, or group, for they can instantly call for a lynching or give someone a pass. Except for one cable television network (Fox), the television news media march in lock step. If one gives a person a pass, they all give him a pass. If one lynches the target, they all applaud the lynching and join in.

Intimidation by political correctness works along these lines. Should someone without thinking of the retaliation call a pig a pig, or with forethought, say to himself, "Hey, that is a pig, and by golly I'm going to call it a pig"; the immediate response is not to clean up the pig, but to respond with "racist," "bigot," "lunatic fringe," "redneck," et cetera. That signals to the media that you did not like the guy calling your pig a pig, and depending on who you are (Republicans or Independents need not apply), the mass media will pick up the chant and drive it home. Clearly it doesn't matter in the least if the pig is a pig. What matters is that someone wanted to suppress free speech and free thought in order to prevent others from telling the truth about you or your interests. After all, if enough people called your pig a pig, the rest of the country might join in and say, "Why, of course that is a pig. It's as plain as the nose on your face."

Political correctness, however, is not an equal opportunity undertaking. For all practical purposes, political correctness is only a requirement of the straight white male. Groups bearing a government approved "minority" status are exempt from political correctness requirements. The reason for the invention of political correctness is that there are some things that some people, usually a member of a minority, do not want to hear you say. Although what you say might be true, mostly true, or your opinion about them, they are so fearful of the truth or just your opinion, they cannot bear to face it. Of course, they apparently don't subscribe to the words "and the truth will set you free." In reality, if one cannot or will not face the truth anytime there is a problem, that problem can never be corrected. Political correctness is counterproductive to good change, for it stifles debate. If one cannot talk about something, he cannot debate it. If he cannot debate it, he cannot isolate the issue or problem. Finally, if he cannot isolate the issue, he cannot correct it.

One of the ironies of this practice (and it clearly pinpoints the heart of the matter) is that each and every day, news organizations and newspapers put forth their opinions of countless matters without being attacked by their peers. So the fear is purely the subject matter that some minority refuses to face. It is an everyday fact that Christianity or the straight white male can be ridiculed, made the butt of jokes, denigrated, mocked, or whatever. No issue of political correctness here. The reason, of course, is that the mass media not only approve of this practice, they lead the charge in conducting this disgraceful act. The mass media is not about to charge itself with political incorrectness.

Once a man is charged with political incorrectness by the media, the group that has taken offense will threaten to boycott or some like action, until they get the punishment they have selected. Usually, that is dismissal from whatever job the off ending guy holds.

Most folk are aware of the killing of thirteen people and the wounding of thirty others last fall by an army officer in the heart of our country. No, this wasn't your run-of-the-mill WECSMM (white, European, Christian, straight, mostly male) officer, this was an Islamic officer of Arab extraction. After hearing of the horrible incident on television and before the officer's name was revealed, I told my wife exactly who it probably was, except his name was unknown. Well, so far as I know, it is not illegal for me to profile. And that folks, is part of the decay of the once great U.S. This guy, as the reports go, apparently did not want the be assigned to the Mideast, where he would be part of a military force deployed against his brother Arabs and his brother Muslims. Other things that weren't going his way, so he just went out on a temper tantrum and kills thirteen (so far) and wounded thirty others. Now, as soon as this guy recovers from his wounds, the only chance of him getting justice is in a military court. However, before that happens, I suspect the ACLU or a first year Harvard law student, or possibly Iran, will intervene on his behalf and demand that he be tried in the civilian court mess. I can see it already.

Even before the bodies were in their graves, the mass media exposed their position—he was under stress, he had been kidded about his religion, he was against the war. Clearly they are in the mass murder's court; haven't heard them identify with the victims or the families of the victims once. Now the military apparently paid for this guy to go to medical school. From the various reports, it appears a clear case of political correctness. The guy was where he was because the Army was unable to call a pig a pig.

As information continues to come in on this Islamic killer, it becomes pretty clear that had he been a WECSM (white, European, Christian, straight male), he would have been expelled from the Army long ago. But this guy fell into the protected-species slot. This automatically invokes political correctness and "hate" speech protection. You are clearly a prejudiced person if you even hint that this guy is an extremist, or perhaps a person that is unfit, even dangerous, for the service. You are the guilty person, the person to be watched and cashiered, because no way could it be one of their protected species of minorities. There is even a report that despite a less than stellar fitness report, the guy was promoted to major. Probably some WECSM looking to improve his fitness report by meeting some "diversity" goal. Political correctness is obviously a dangerous form of denial of free speech, for one is unable to call a pig a pig. Should one dare to call a pig a pig, however, he better not call the pig a fat pig or nasty pig or slop pig. Then he *would* get it with both barrels.

In a review, or "investigation," of the Fort Hood murders, two civilian democrat political appointees assigned to the Pentagon left out religion, ethnic origin, background, even the name of the killer, stating that these factors were not relevant. To repeat an early observation, democrats never learn from past errors. Their motto: Long live political correctness, diversity, and affirmative action. Their attitude: To hell with the country.

Those of you with a long memory will remember that it was the liberals and the courts that facilitated so many foreigners into our country, to the point it is no longer our country. This very minute the television news is reporting that a man of Hispanic origins gunned down one person and wounded five others. Apparently he felt that he wasn't being treated as well as he thought he deserved.

WHERE AND WHEN DID POLITICAL CORRECTNESS BEGIN?

I do not know the precise answer to that question for I have not kept records on the new phrases and the list of forbidden words. Only memory points to the northeast mass media outlets and I believe the first two words on the political correctness list were the Q and the N word - see even today one is intimidated into not spelling them out. Very quickly other words made the list- secretary, janitor, custodian, yard boy, fat legs or fat derriere, ethnic origin tags, and strange convoluted phrasing began to appear and ethic jokes disappeared. The latest of these is the phrase "undocumented immigrant". For the uninformed that is politically correct speak for "illegal alien" and it does sound sweeter does it not. But it only masks the crime; it doesn't make it go away. Ethnic origin jokes even made the "No-No" list such that today one never hears a Polish joke. Shame on us.

How far down the path of political correctness have we traveled – more that most citizens believe. Before I retired there was a Human Resource (formerly Personnel) Department individual in my office. At some point I casually referred to a group of females as "the girls." Changing the direction of the conversation he came out with "you can't call them that". To which I naively said "What". His response was that I could refer to them as women, ladies or females, but I could not call them girls. Let that soak in for a few minutes before continuing.

I strongly suspect; however, had I referred to a group of males as "the guys" I would have had no comment about that. "Girls" is apparently on the politically correct forbidden list while "guys" is not on the list. Can you figure that one ? In all my years of referring to the girls as "the girls" I have never had a single one object; at least to my face. I suspect that is at least in part because I almost never say those words in other then a gentlemanly manner and not a derogatory manner. Could it be that the reason that the northeast has to resort to political correctness is that they have to deal with so many people that are not gentlemen or ladies. Be assured, down South a girl can be a girl and still be a first class lady and I thank the southern girls for their class.

There is another word, the "R" word (meaning rednecks) that is not on the politically correct forbidden list. The reason for that is that rednecks are not one of the protected species, therefore the media motor mouths and the New York columnists, are quick to play that card. But from the rednecks one gets a totally different reaction for he is just as likely to spit a mouthful of tobacco in the media mouths face and say "Thank you, that is the nicest thing anyone has said to me all day," climb in his ole pickup truck and go on about his business. Now I would never think of doing this or even suggest it to someone else, but if the label "redneck" were directed to a serious man from the Avery Island area who was intent on living up to the full measure of what a northern media motor mouth (NMMM) expected of him he may take his middle finger suitably enlarged and elongated by a proboscis which he wrapped with course sandpaper liberally (pardon the pun) garnished with Tabasco, jalapeno and/or habanera and flash the name caller. Just the thought of such an experience should ensure that any halfway intelligent person would never utter the "R" word again. See we pulled that off without even getting a media motor mouth involved.

I do not normally wear T-shirts with messages on them but one year when we were all on a ski trip to Breckenridge the kids purchased me a T-shirt which I do wear from time to time. I thought it was kinda cute and an "in your face" to liberals. The message on the back of the shirt reads "Danger – Redneck Skier."

What is really queer about the PC gang is that the words that are on my verboten list are the 4-8 letter words normally only to be spoken by a sailor are all perfectly fine with them, whereas the normal everyday words I find perfectly acceptable are on their "no-no" list. One of us is out of line and I have a hunch it is the PC gang for without the loud mouth of the liberal media America could no more hear their chatter then mine.

I have only met one real live national TV news man. This was at a media charm school in New York years ago. This guy seemed nice enough but was 100% programmed to stand by the media news broadcast as accurate and without bias. This individual has since passed away. I have never met the media mouths of today nor have I ever met any of the History Channel Louisiana Alligator hunters. In case you have never seen the program it is a live documentary of a day or days in the lives of these Louisiana swamp people that make part of their living hunting alligators. So clearly I have never met any of these people and have only seen them on TV. But if I were to spend some time with any of these people I had rather spend two weeks with the Louisiana alligator hunters than I had 4 hours with the media motor mouths (Fox excluded).

After all one cannot expect too much from a redneck. He has not had the necessary training in etiquette to be able to walk off the set with dignity when the guest raised the debate stakes and the heat gets too great. Now that takes great skill. And yet even with all their training and skills the girls storming of the set with Bill O'Reilly as a guest still appear as narrow minded, empty hotheads. While they may appear that way to some, to me that is exactly what they are. Actually now that I think about that expensive charm school in New York; they short changed us. They never once trained us in the technique of storming off the set when the heat got too hot for our small brains. Of course, there is always the possibility that the walk out was an orchestrated event directed to ratings improvements, after all, anything for ratings.

SPORTS POLITICAL CORRECTNESS

As I recall one of the early flaps by the P.C. Gestapo was the sport team mascots and in some cases chants. Out of the woodwork they came with all manner of objections. In some cases it was the Indians; for the University of Mississippi it was Colonel Reb. For the university to ditch a popular mascot in the name of political correction was an unpopular, long and unpleasant process with most people declining to participate. Those that did vote chose to replace Colonel Reb with a bear, a black bear. Perhaps the reader can see the connection for no one down here could. I suggested if they were going to ditch Colonel Reb that they replace him with Elmer Fudd or perhaps his fellow actor, the Wabbit. Well, perhaps not; but they could always call themselves the Zeros. That way no one could possibly be offended except perhaps some math professor from a northeast "prestige" school.

THE "K" WORD

This is so politically incorrect. My lovely wife's ancestors came to this country from Ulm, Germany many years ago. There have been times in our 54 year marriage when I have felt compelled to say something to the effect..... Do I have to use the "K" or the PC police come after me if I say kraut.... oh, heck, I'm going to just say it.... "That you know the kraut in you is showing itself." Anyone harmed by my saying that? Certainly not my gentle bride of many years, she just throws her chest out because she's proud of our ancestors. I can't even offend her when I do my very best to;

she just says "darn right and proud of it." A guy cannot win. She will not even cooperate when I am trying my best to put her in her place! I'm sure at this point the reader can see that I am completely justified in using the K word. Sounds silly, yep, but that his political correctness - silly, outrageous and criminal for the objective is to deny one his freedom of speech.

POLITICAL CORRECTNESS AND BIASED REPORTING FOSTERS IGNORANCE

Besides rednecks there are other things uniquely southern that one will not find on the politically correct "NO-NO" list for they do not offend the sensitive protected species. These other things included mocking or mimicking the southern manners of speech (for whites only), put down of the southern schools, jokes of living in the swamp with snakes, spiders and alligators, and sometimes the use of two names e.g. Peggy Sue or Bubba which the northern media identifies as the generic given name for a redneck.

A couple of personal stories will highlight the erroneous northern perception of the South. Some years ago my children's dad was asked to come to Pennsylvania to help in an accident recovery situation. So the family moved to Pennsylvania. The youngest son and the youngest daughter attended Hersey High which we found to be a good school. Generally the other kids left my youngest son alone, but the youngest daughter, who was a lovely southern Belle was hounded. She was a senior at Hershey high. Many of the students just could not nor would not get past her "southern drawl" as described by a northerner. My wife and I were in bed one night when the two kids came in after a football game and the daughter just flung herself across our bed sobbing. We were startled; no, alarmed. She said some of the kids just would not stop hounding her about her manner of speech, about the south, etc. etc. She begged me to let her go back home and finish with the class she had been with since first grade. And so we did. We packed up her things and over Christmas brought her back home so she could finish with her class. She was a happy little girl. The youngest son adapted to the environment.

In some ways my eldest son experienced this northern attitude to southerners. He transferred to Penn State when we moved. During his college time he dated a little girl nearby. On his first date with the girl he had time to speak with her father as she finished dressing. At that time my son had traveled extensively in the states and had been abroad once. The father opened the conversation with something to the fact of "aren't you glad to be up here so you can get a decent education. Aren't you glad to get away from the snakes, alligators and bugs and so on". It was almost if the man expected my son to be barefoot, in overalls, a tattered straw hat, and there to pick up his daughter with a mule and wagon. My son being the gentleman he was, simply asked the girl's father had he ever been south. The response was an immediate "of course, we have been down to Maryland several times". And, my son let it go at that. He kindly did not point out that to get to the Gulf of Mexico, which is where we have lived since moving from South Carolina, one had an 18 hour drive due South all the way. And truthfully one could hardly fault the man for his ignorance; after all he was just the victim of the biased northern press and television. Since he had never personally been south of Maryland he had to get his mental picture of the South from another source - the northern press. Although this type of misinformation is not critical to the country; providing misinformation to the public, North or South, is a crime for the citizens are rendered unable to make intelligent decisions. And even at this date when one would have thought the northern media outlets would have outgrown their infantile conduct we still have to watch the one and only "fair and balanced" station well into the 21st century. Another shame on our nation. I have been in all 50 of the states that make up the United States and be assured the South has no corner on the market when it comes to rednecks, ignorance or prejudice.

WHAT IS A DEMOCRAT?

Some people consider the words democrat and democratic synonymous. Therefore, throughout this little book I have tried to make a distinction. To me, "democratic" is a lofty and praiseworthy word, although a mite impractical. The word "democrat," conversely, is an ugly word today. Should the word *democratic* be used in this book, it will be italicized to make the distinction.

Basic definitions of a democrat: a person that can spot a wart on George W. Bush's nose at five hundred yards, yet standing three feet from Bill Clinton can't see that he is one.

A democrat is a person that will ask for the definition of "is" or "if" or "sex" or "lie" with a perfectly straight face, while all the time chuckling inside at his ingenuity.

A democrat is a person that will boldly throw out a solution (or two) for every problem known to man, without the slightest idea of how to implement his solution nor the consequences. Shoot first, aim later. Note the White House in action since January 2009.

Is a person that sees no evil except in the person who disagrees with him. To him, George W. Bush is evil personified. Rush, Sarah, Sean, Glenn. See the news media.

Is a person that has a burning desire to take your money and give it to the "poor," but would never do so with their own millions. I understand they feel their millions would not be enough to go around; therefore, they expect the public to cover the poor with their money. One doesn't have to look far to see a bunch of people out there with great wealth that was bestowed on them or was acquired with little or no effort, beating the drums for the "poor." Is that how they solve their guilt complex, by being a hero in the eyes of the poor and the media? That sounds pretty reasonable to me.

Is a person that cries out for freedom of expression in word and deed, yet will stop at nothing to prevent anyone expressing a different position. Again, a one way street mentality.

Is a person that looks at any social problem, from education, to morals, to crime, and says it will be just fine if the government would send more money. For heaven's sake, let's not look at the real root of the problem. We might come up with an answer that is not politically correct. That is, the democrats would not like to hear the answer.

Is a person that believes you are only entitled to protect yourself, your family, and your property from assault after you can prove the perpetuator intends you harm—like after you are dead, for example. Consider the ruling that if someone kills a burglar coming in a window and he falls in the house, you are a victim defending yourself. Yet if he falls outside the house, *he* becomes the victim. Same situation, but role reversal based on some judge totally lacking in judgment.

Is a person who, along with Caroline Kennedy, can't understand why the magic of the Kennedy name failed to secure a senate seat for her. After all, it worked for two of her uncles, the younger of which had zero qualifications for the job, other than, of course, his last name.

Is a person that still worships the Kennedy idol, even though he has been gone for almost fifty years. Of course, they are in the same ballpark as almost all of the media.

Is a person that would support a cabinet appointment for the brother of a Democrat president (nepotism), but would throw sixteen tantrums should the same situation exist in a Republican administration. Democrats have a one way street mentality.

Is a person that would understand that the purple robe of the Kennedy name only extends to those relatives whose last name is Kennedy. Even though some relatives have the exact same position in the Kennedy clan, but do not bear the Kennedy name ...Well, they are just like the rest of us. No covering by the purple robe. Sorry.

Is a person that would never, ever acknowledge that it was Lyndon B. Johnson who flung open the door to the social and economic disaster we live in today. All John Kennedy did was barely crack the door. Johnson opened the door that permitted the media and the courts to wreak havoc with our country.

Is a person that would agree with one newspaper that proclaimed, less than a week after the inauguration of Barack Hussein Obama that we had entered Camelot II. Personally, I never saw a Camelot. I must have slept through that one.

Is a person that operates primarily from emotion, while an independent or conservative operates primarily from the brain. Now, there is a time and place for emotions, but not in politics. Is a person that would not understand that the word combinations of "liberal democrat" and "radical democrat" are double negatives.

Is a person that is, at the very least, a left-wing liberal, runs for election as a moderate, and runs up his true skull and crossbones radical flag as soon as he gets sworn into office. Take, for example, Hillary's infamous health care plan, Obama's "some members of my family are Muslims," or Obama's spending bill made up of fifty years of wild democrat schemes that never saw the light of day previously.

Is a person that sees nothing wrong with frolicking with a young girl in the Oval Office cloakroom while attempting to abridge the constitutional right of Americans to bear arms. One might say his left hand was on the trigger and his right hand was on her ... Well, you get the picture.

Is a person that sees no wrong in releasing scores and scores of convicted felons from prison in the last days of his term—especially if there is or has been financial benefits. Got to make a living somehow, and he knew he would get a pass by the media.

Is a person that can't see a commander in chief failing in his sworn duties to protect this country and its citizens (Jimmy Carter and Bill Clinton), yet crucifies one that does so (George W. Bush). No room for jokes here.

Is a person that will not answer a direct question if he knows that if he does, he is going to look like a fool. Instead, he will discuss the weather, the latest fashions, his favorite television shows, or simply go on the attack. In short, he will say or do anything rather than answer the direct question. This, of course, includes questions that only require a *yes* or a *no*, or a *true* or *false*. Have to save face, you know. After all it is more important than saving honor. Of course, honor is an element of character, and we already know a democrat doesn't believe in character. Prior to Bill Clinton and Hillary, it was already known by any thinking person that the liberals had long ago trashed character as of no value. Take a look at their track record.

But faced with the ultimate showdown for the party president, liberals were forced to come right and say it, and in fact they did just that. They said character doesn't matter. It's the job getting done.

We know this is the democrat thinking, for in the past sixty years there has been a constant attack on the character and nature of the population. Mostly gradual and incremental, but still an assault. Since BC, the gradual has changed to a full-blown assault on the national character, to the point that it has made a dramatic shift downward.

In keeping with that attitude, data on how many people still say they believe in God or that regularly attend worship services notwithstanding, the national character is clearly secular.

Well, BC, HC, BHO, and all your democrats need to stand by for a news flash. Character counts. Not only does character count, but it is one of the factors, or possibly the top factor, that determines the success or failure of the republic. Understand I am not referring to a single person, be it BC or BHO, for they are as nothing. It is the national character to which I refer. National character is what defined this country in its glory years.

Is a person that doesn't understand change in its classic sense. The media and some elements in our society, over a long period, successfully brainwashed the public into equating change with the words good, desirable, or beneficial. They have even gone so far as to state and restate the obvious—"things are going to change," which obviously is true. But in its classic sense, change can be good, bad, or even indifferent. What, of course, the media and these elements want you to believe is that the changes they advocate are good by definition! When pigs fly. Actually, if you do not subscribe to their proposals, you are labeled a reactionary or not progressive.

Is a person that believes (at least pretends to believe) that the answer to all of his problems can be corrected very simply. Send money. When that doesn't correct the problem, it is because you failed to send enough money. Our public education institutions are classic examples of that mentality. Been there, done that; it doesn't work.

Is a person that has a one way street mentality. What is not suitable for them, they label as unfair and mean-spirited. The inevitable outcome of one-way streets is that one cannot turn around and go back to reality.

Is a person that gives a lawyer credit for getting a double murderer off the hook, when in fact it was the jury that let him off the hook. Actually, I could have been the murderer's lawyer and that same jury would have let him off the hook. The jury might have taken longer in its deliberations as to how in the world it was going to justify its decision. The jurors might have started with, "Let's try 'there was not a shadow of a doubt.' But wait; there is one too many words in that sentence. How about we drop "not" to make it a lucky seven words for the defendant?

Is a person that would not understand why a Southerner would vote against a fellow Southerner from Georgia who was running for president. You may not recall the campaign, but I still do. When faced with a question he knew he couldn't answer without showing his true colors, the candidate simply gave a three to five minute monologue. He would vocalize a mass of words without saying anything. Jimmy, the democrats and media still love you!

Is a person that believed the national media when they discredited the stories coming out of Arkansas, when Bill was running for president, that he had a history of entertaining the ladies and vice versa. In the light of subsequent events, is it just possible that the stories could be true? I believe the stories were true. The national media knew they were true and lied to their audiences, because Bill was their man and they would have denied their own mother (I know you not) to secure the election for him. Wait a minute. Did we not just have a repeat of that scenario, with the media campaigning for their boy once again? They put him in office; therefore, it will be impossible for them to criticize him. Barack Hussein Obama, you are in way over your head.

Is a person that would never see the Chicago/Illinois connection. It's the home of the Daley machine, the machine that gave Kennedy the presidency; the locale of the infamous St. Valentine's Day massacre; the former home of some of the most violent criminals in U.S. history; the place where a double murderer fled for succor; the home of Reverend Wright; the home of the former governor, Rod Blagojevich; and we don't want to omit BHO and MO.

Is a person that can preach lofty ideals, morals, and ethics, except where it pertains to his own house. Then they can make a few exceptions here and there, because he "has unique qualifications," or he is "the *only* guy that can do the job," et cetera. No matter that he is a tax cheat, because it was only an honest mistake. Please; using the term "mistake" taxes (excuse the pun) our belief mechanism. And using the term "honest" puts penalty and interest on our taxed belief. Excuse me, did I say something wrong?

Are people that, usually, cannot take care of themselves. They must have some form of government aid. Think about it. The help may come in various forms—financial help, preferential treatment in hiring, preferential treatment in layoff s, preferential treatment in admission to some schools, laws that criminalize someone for looking at them cross-eyed, help in housing, hospital care, electric bill assistance, phone bill help, acquiring loans for homes they cannot pay back, and laws that penalized someone who commits a so-called hate crime. Aren't almost all violent crimes hate crimes?

Is a person that would never think of the straight white male as the only segment of the population that is not labeled as some sort of minority. That's right. The entire rest of the national population is some type of minority, except the straight white male. It is the only segment of the population that the media can ridicule, can poke fun at for its eccentricities and idiosyncrasies and sometimes ridiculous behavior, and not be guilty of that unforgivable sin, political incorrectness. The straight white male is not going to send in hate mail, picket the studios, scream in the broadcasters' faces, spit at them, write his congressman, nor intimidate or boycott the media. And that is because he wants no government help to stand (or fall) on his own two feet, and he is man enough to consider the inferiority of the source. After all, they are mostly democrats that must have government aid because they can't make it on their own.

Is a person that will give his party candidate or elected official a pass on any and all the sins and crimes in the world, so long as the candidate supports the party line and doesn't cut welfare benefits. Sure, why not.

Is a person that may support the national well-being and safety somewhere down the line after all his itches (does it bring in votes?) have been taken cared for. It's all about priorities I am priority one.

Is a person that feels that four-letter words are okay, the more the better, while believing that *civil* and *civilized* are dirty words. That's right, stop, look and listen.

Is a person that will whine for or support so-called "reparations." For heaven's sake, what do they think has been taking place ever since Lyndon Johnson flung open the Treasury doors and started the printing presses rolling? That is going on fifty years of "reparations," and it hasn't done any noticeable good. In fact, it has made matters worse for much of the welfare population. The government welfare programs are countless. With all of this largess, one would think that was plenty for anyone. That doesn't even take into consideration the countless private charities directed primarily or exclusively at minorities. With all of this gratis, why would one work?

Is a person that would never notice that when Kennedy was running for president, the media came out loud and clear: religion does not matter. But when Mitt Romney was running, it was a different but subtle approach. They never came out and rejected this guy for his religious views. No, they just kept it on the discussion table day after day, until the public got the impression that there must be something wrong here, or else the media would have dismissed it. I call it murder by innuendo.

Is a person that would support John Kennedy's definition of a liberal: a person that looks forward, not backward. To a degree, even I would agree. However, the flaw here is that a person who refuses to look backward is condemned to never learn from the errors of the past. Come to think of it, that pretty well defines a democrat.

A NOTE ON PUBLIC SCHOOLS

A few years back, my lovely daughter had started her first year of teaching. She was in a nearby city, and started out teaching the fifth grade. Shortly after the start of the school year, she called and asked if I were available to tutor some of her students in math a couple of days a week. This was a mostly minority school. I started out with hope in my heart at the opportunity to make a difference for the better in these kids' lives. It only took a few weeks for me to get my feet back on the ground.

After repeated attempts, I found I could not teach these kids fifth grade math. I so advised my sweet daughter, and in a meeting with the school principal, I told her she could never teach these kids fifth grade math because they did not know third grade math. They did not know their multiplication tables. Assignments were not completed—the dog ate it, I forgot, I left it at home, I was too busy, et cetera. With an exception or two, they did not want to learn. I believe they knew they were not where they should be and were discouraged. I also told the principal that if the school system felt it was doing these kids a favor by promoting them each year regardless of their performance (supposedly to avoid damaging their self-esteem), the school system was dead wrong. People felt good about themselves when they did something good and they were successful. All the school system was doing was building up a huge bow wave that would doom these kids to a unfulfilled life. Then you have some big time loss of self-esteem. I did find out, however, that the kids were good at finger painting and knowing their "rights." Responsibility? What is that?

One more personal tale before moving on to the democrats. When my grandchild graduated from high school last year, I was once again astonished at the distribution of intelligence in this graduating class of several hundred. Five or six kids graduated with highest honors. About 15–20 percent achieved high honors, and about 20–25 percent graduated with honors. I could be wrong, but I believe the classic distribution curve is still valid here. If that's true, the school systems are cheating on the students and we know they are. Based on what little I know of today's rationale, I assume once again they are front-loading the grades to help the kids feel better about themselves and to make themselves look good. Wrong, wrong, wrong!

Democrats refuse to come to terms with *the* problem with the public education system today. They can't because the answer is too painful for them to face. Instead they resort to the tired (if not true) path. We don't have enough money. Some states now spend well over half of all their income on schools. We know there will never be enough money simply because money is not the problem. Still, schools seem always to get more money, because the legislators that are fellow travelers cannot face the real problem either. Therefore, the schools automatically get their vote. Couple that with some legislators' fear of facing the wrath of the teachers' union, or the fear of appearing to be against better education, and presto, you have a prescription for instant money. It goes without saying that the severity of the public education problem varies with one's location in the country, as well as whether the school is in a city or outside a city. Demographics at work.

The state in which I live is the poorest of the poor. Yet there was a day when it had excellent school systems staffed with teachers that made maybe $2,000.00 a year. These school systems turned out students equipped to become successful applicants to West Point and Annapolis; to become successful businessmen; presidents or vice presidents of national and international companies; as well as educators, editors, doctors, writers, lawyers, poets, and captains and generals; such as Fox Conner, mentor to Eisenhower when Eisenhower was posted to Panama. And these schools used a passing grade of 75, not 65, or 50, or no grade at all.

These schools were able to perform this feat of education not because they had all the bucks they wanted, but because the teachers were competent and the school system provided them with an environment that permitted them to do their job. Actually, it was no feat of education in those days. It was just taking care of business. There was essentially no discipline problem, because the school system did not tolerate bad behavior and the kids knew it. The schools were safe. This was in the golden years of the country, before the courts, lawyers, and media stuck their cancerous hands into the education stew. In those days, the school superintendents were not in a race to offer more courses to highlight 168 courses to beef up their résumé. The core curriculum was the focal point in high schools, and it was keyed with those courses required throughout the earlier school years. Elective courses were limited, and students did not receive credit for courses whose subjects or activities that were considered extracurricular. Huge numbers of elective courses and credit for extracurricular activities not only detract from the core curriculum, but they cost big bucks and the data show the system is broken. In that day so long ago, at assembly the children sang such songs as "My Country, 'Tis of Thee, sweet land of liberty" and "America the Beautiful," and the children were not harmed. In fact, they were helped. Nor did they grow up to be a bunch of fanatics bent on establishing a state-sponsored religion, or to overthrow the government. That was left to others' imaginations.

PROFILING

It is common perception that democrats, or people that usually vote democrat, come from the following population segments:

1. A very high percentage of people employed in the mass media, especially television writers and programmers; newspaper publishers, editors, and writers (hopefully this segment will soon self-destruct); magazine editors, et cetera are democrats.
2. A very high percentage of homosexuals are democrats.
3. Essentially all blacks are democrats.
4. A very high percentage of schoolteachers and administrators are democrats.
5. A very high percentage of college professors are democrats, perhaps approaching 100 percent of those in the "social" or non-scientific areas. May want to think about that also (hence the youth inclination).
6. A very high percentage of trial lawyers and judges are democrats. Of course, except for a few lower level judges, all judges are lawyers. Hence the mess in our legal system.
7. Most handicapped individuals are democrats.
8. Far more white females than white and straight males are democrats, or at least vote democrat.
9. Most people of Jewish origins are democrats.
10. Most people of Mexican origins are democrats.
11. You are probably a democrat if you live in any city in the U.S. with a population of 250,000 or greater. You are probably not a liberal if you live outside those cities. And that tells you something about our cities. Take Oregon for example. The voting record for Oregon (pre-2008) is conservative outside the population centers and liberal in the population centers. Thus the vast areas of the state are conservative, and only a comparatively few acres are liberal.

The courts, on some vague argument, have ruled that profiling is illegal. It is still practiced in many areas, but only in those areas sanctioned by the minorities and the media. BHO did it when he uttered his infamous, "[they] acted stupidly" remark. The police routinely do it when they say we are looking for a white male, unmarried, living alone, and was cruel to animals at an early age. Politicians and pollsters do it every day. A traffic stop by the highway patrol to check driver's licenses, inspection stickers, et cetera, could be considered profiling according to the courts' argument, because innocent people by the droves are stopped. Profiling makes sense for the police, for schools, for hiring, and for the military, and the courts are once again out in left field for making it illegal.

DEMOCRAT IQ GAP

Shortly after the media put their guy in the White House in 2009, he appointed another minority member as his Attorney General. This guy immediately started whining about race relations. Although, I did not hear his remarks, it is understood that some (or all) of them were aimed at race relations on weekends. Apparently they are okay during the workweek, when the government (at all levels) has a big stick to enforce their rules. But on weekends when the government, at least for now, has no such rules of conduct and therefore no budget, it becomes a segregated society again. I understand he also said something about Americans being cowards when it came to discussing race relations.

There are at least two points here that beg for "the rest of the story." First, it doesn't take an IQ of 133 to figure out where this guy is going to direct the federal police force. I can see it coming even now: a Supreme Court ruling that separate but equal weekends are clearly unconstitutional, and that you white folk have until Friday at 5 pm to get an affirmative action plan in place, so that there will be proportional representation at all weekend parties, ball games, cookouts, et cetera. The federal police will take the names of those failing to meet their quotas. Of course, this ruling will apply only to the southeastern states. Please do not snicker. Such a ruling is no more far-fetched than many other court decisions. Some of you may recall that Lincoln's proclamation only applied to the Southern states. Some voting laws, likewise, apply only in the South.

The second point is that this guy must have an IQ of fewer than three digits if he doesn't realize that it is the minorities that do not want to discuss why that is mostly a true statement. At his level in government, he should realize it has nothing to do with the color of one's skin. If he doesn't know that, he should be sent to Chicago or institutionalized.

Now that I think about it, this guy and his boss may not break a three digit IQ combined. I'm confident that even the daughter of the thirty-ninth president (who, incidentally, had a little problem dealing with Iran) knew exactly what the response should be to a message from the White House to Tehran that said, in essence, "Let's get together, hold hands, sing songs, plant pansies [or is it patsies], make peace signs, and smoke dope." BHO got what he unwittingly asked for with both barrels right in the crotch. He clearly needs a caretaker. The media sold his line to a gullible American public, but Tehran doesn't deal in snake oil.

The thirty-ninth president tried snake oil for 444 days without selling a single drop; whereas it took a Republican man only a few minutes to correct the problem, and all he promised was a hell of a beating. Now the democrats just won't talk about this. In fact, it is impossible for them to find it in their minds; it is blocked out. And if there is anything a liberal hates more than a straight white male, it is the military. That force, or the threat of force, could solve anything is far beyond their comprehension. The liberal is far more in tune with a sneak attack involving innocent people and civilian property against their own country, than uniformed military action against an enemy. Don't try to figure this out if your brain functions in the logic mode.

OUR FAILED LEGAL SYSTEM

In the paper distributed locally, there was a story of a Tulane University student who answered the doorbell of his apartment. He was murdered by two people looking for money. As it turned out, the mother of the two testified that they were looking for cigarette money. Not even in your home, are you safe, not even for a pack of cigarettes.

In the newspaper recently I read that tale of a man who had stolen over

$15,000. The article stated the exact amount—$15,694.34. The man was sentenced to eighteen months and ordered to repay the money, down to the penny. Now please compare that with the high rollers stealing hundreds of millions, or even billions, of dollars. I cannot recall one single case in recent years where the conviction of a high roller was followed by a requirement to pay full restitution. Not one. It will be interesting to see what the courts will award the Stanford guy from Houston who only stole $8 billion. It has been reported that Madoff has a net worth of only $823 million, (with only $17 million in cash). Now most folks would think that was pretty serious bucks, but not if one has stolen $50, $65, or $80 billion, whatever the correct figure is. Why, $823 million is hardly more than pocket change. He was sentenced to a suitable prison term, but please stand by to see if he is ordered to pay full restitution, as the poor guy who only stole the $15,000 plus change. Not a chance in $823 million. As for me, the net worth of the Madoff s and Stanfords of the world is a pile of cow manure. The same net worth is shared by the Enron, WorldCom, Tyco, et cetera executives that stole their employee pension funds. No hole is too deep to bury such vermin.

It has been reported that prior to the Bank of America takeover of Merrill Lynch, Merrill Lynch paid out $3.6 billion to employees in bonuses. Bank of America has received public money in the bailout scheme. Now AIG is also guilty, but it only paid out $450 million. AIG is a recipient of public bailout bucks. Somehow I have the feeling that if John Doe were to try this scam, he would be hustled off by the Feds to the big house. Again, these people are the high rollers and above the normal rules, regulations, laws, and judges John Doe has to deal with.

Another case, similar to one referenced earlier but with a vastly different outcome, will show the injustice of our legal system. This person embezzled $60,873, and was also convicted and sentenced. This person was ordered, and properly so, to repay the money in full, yet was sentenced only to two years house arrest. So how can a person convicted of a $15,000 crime come out with eighteen months in prison? Multiply these examples reported locally nationwide, and one can see the horrible inequities across our nation. Compound that conflict with the drug, assault, et cetera crimes with multiple arrests, three, four, five, up to eighteen times, with no such sentence, and it leaves a person scratching his head. I see it as a failure to have an anchor or benchmark. From the Supreme Court on down to the lower courts—I believe this is a national problem—judges are interpreting the Constitution or the laws according to other own biases and political leanings; in effect duplicating the chaos of the French Revolution, in which every citizen did what was okay in his own mind. Of course, if your mind differed from that of the council, it was off with your head. For the democrat readers that have come this far, you may want to read the details of that event. But then again, you don't like to hear "the rest of the story," do you?

In this area, we have a constant problem with criminals who are out on probation continuing to pursue criminal activities. A prime example was recently reported. Seems this guy has been caught and jailed eighteen times, which is, I suspect, one tenth of the total of 180 criminal activities he has been engaged in. Seems he was convicted of distributing crack cocaine and received a ten-year suspended sentence. He has been arrested seven times while on probation, the latest being for aggravated assault with a firearm. He is accused of shooting someone in the stomach. This will be his *third hearing* to *discuss revoking probation*. Sounds impossible, but not so. It is entirely possible and highly likely, should one read the convoluted court rational for treatment of criminals. For example, arrest on non-felony charges and some felony charges doesn't mean it is legally proper or *moral* to revoke probation; or—get this now—higher courts (including the Supreme Court) have ruled it unreasonable to deny probation for a "minor" offense if an alternative to prison is available. An alternative to prison is always a possibility! As I stated earlier, the entire legal system is broken beyond repair. The judge in this case is on a high plane (not necessarily a rational plane, but a high plane!) for he has taken the position that "judicial ethics" stop him from speaking of the case outside the courtroom. How dare he speak of ethics with a straight face.

That the legal system is a wreck is without doubt true, and it can be attributed to one main failing: It has no anchor to guide it. Although the Constitution was supposed to do that, it long ago was trashed by the judges themselves. The executive and legislative branches have sat on their respective backsides and allowed it to happen, as the federal courts agreed to start looking at trivial cases and cases better left to the state courts. Today the Supreme Court has no checks and balances on it, as do the other two branches of government. As envisioned by our Founding Fathers, this perfect system has failed due to an overly aggressive court system and weak checks by the other two branches of government. Once the Supreme Court has spoken (frequently on a 5/4 split, which reveals it is a questionable opinion), everyone falls on their faces, bows, and says, "Yes, master." The remote appointment process, especially requiring Senate confirmation, is of little or no effect, except in possibly getting a person of somewhat known political leaning. But how he will rule on court cases is beyond anyone's wildest imagination. The lower courts get the same blind obedience at their level as the Supreme Court. In my opinion, there are times when the chief executive should say "Get lost," but no. The Court can put demands on the other two branches, while they can or will do nothing to the Court. Think about that power: raw and wrong. Again, in some cases the chief executive should simply tell the Court that its ruling is not even remotely related to the Constitution of the U.S. Many courts have been allowed to make laws in the form of court decisions. Other than possibly the television, nothing in this country has more power, and that power is routinely abused.

A prime example of where the Supreme Court has gone astray is the First Amendment, regarding freedom of speech. The Courts has gone way beyond anything to do with speech. It has allowed all manner of conduct, acts, and even objects to stand in as some form of speech, even if they are not even remotely connected to speech. Such wild interpretations have, of course, led to the destruction of the anchor that should have kept the Court as a believable and respected institution. e liberals/democrats rejoice in its ruling more often than not, as it supports their agenda of making things that are wrong seem right, and things that are right seem wrong. The U.S. Supreme Court is bad enough, but couple it with the hundreds and thousands of little and big kingdoms out there, frequently going their own ways with little accountability or oversight. These courts, as previously stated, in effect make laws in the form of court rulings. Wrong, dead wrong. The Supreme Court justices vote their political persuasions, and it would be fair to say that most interpretative Court decisions have a liberal political slant. Liberals love this court environment, for it gives them political power as well as economic power. The many contradictions, vague rationales (that may go the other way tomorrow), the "Let's look at how the Europeans are doing it," are justified by the democrats as progressive, dynamic, and decisions based on today's needs. I call it reckless and irresponsible, to say the least. Except as amended by the states, not one word in the Constitution has changed since the day it was written and adopted. Notwithstanding Bill Clinton's disgraceful act, *is* then still means *is* today.

Some articles have been written recently (at least they came to my attention recently) that some jurists at the highest level in this country have suggested that perhaps it was time they went outside the body of laws and others instruments (such as the Constitution) to deal with legal issues. Specifically mentioned were the legal systems in Europe. This has apparently caused heartburn in some people. But that is probably because they haven't really thought it out. The United States' legal system, as distinguished from the justice system, long ago went outside the Constitution for its interpretation of the laws and conduct. Today it is whoever has the biggest mouth, the most stubbornness, the most committed agenda; in other words, the jurist's own opinions and political views. No one who takes the time to examine almost any high profile issue can deny that. Of course, it goes without saying that some sane opinions come out of the system also. Given the system the courts have created, it will not matter a hill of beans if the country were to add a few opinions here and there that the courts say were based on European laws. Who knows? The country may come out a little ahead when compared with opinions based on personal preferences. In fact, it is possible we could come out ahead with a legal system based on almost any solid base.

Some decisions clearly outside the Constitution and clearly not just (as in justice):
1. Affirmative action
2. "Reverse" discrimination. think about that term and its significance. Were the laws written to serve the purposes of only one segment of the population?
3. More severe punishment for so-called hate acts or speech
4. Abortion legalized. Again, not, clearly not, just
5. Preferential treatment in schools, workplaces, et cetera over more qualified students or workers. Helping one person may be acceptable, but not if it punishes someone else.
6. Preferential treatment of so-called minorities in any and all walks of life
7. Legislating by court rulings
8. Imposing voting regulations on some states only
9. Political influence of First Amendment decisions
10. Rulings violating the Second Amendment
11. Any decision based on political correctness. One concrete example of such decisions is gerrymandering. It had been

illegal until the courts started not only allowing it, but in many cases *ordering* it.

12. Any "two wrongs" decision. E.g., giving one person or group preferential treatment (therefore not equal protection) and with the same opinion taking away another's rights, or punishing a man on the basis of some vague theory about the sins of his father, grandfather, great-grandfather, great-great-grandfather, et cetera. Actually a presumed sin, unproven but lumped in with a societal attribute. Fifty or a hundred years later, the courts decide that individuals can be punished for the conduct of a long-gone society (again, not equal protection). Clearly the courts are not only unconstitutional, but they are unjust.

13. "Creation" decisions. With the assistance of the media, the democrats have convinced the masses that universal health care is a right of everyone, even illegal immigrants. Who says? Since the birth of the nation, universal health care has not been a universal right. So why in 2009 does it become a universal right; and should one listen to the democrats, it is apparently a universal right that can be forced on the people, whether or not they want it. Sound crazy? It is. Now, many of these court decisions are not based on new ground to be plowed, but on turf that has stood for most if not all of our existence; such as abortion, criminal rights, creation of new rights for preferred segments of society, even Lincoln's famous "selectivity" in his proclamation.

The courts have lost their way; they are adrift. When they abandoned the Constitution in their quest to rebuild society into their own image, they created a two-headed monster. First and most important, they have lost their status as part of the checks and balances envisioned in the Constitution, which allowed for three equal branches of government, executive, legislative, and judicial. The Supreme Court has become a dictator from which there is no appeal; for outside the Constitution, one can always come up with a personal opinion and rationalize anything and everything. At the stroke of a pen, the Court can void the work of a five hundred plus member Congress, or with the same pen nullify any act of the chief executive, and by a 5/4 vote, no less.

The courts have injected themselves, or allowed themselves to be sucked into every crevice of our society. This is facilitated by an infinite number of lawyers intent on lining their pockets, no matter the cost to society or to individuals. The courts have decided that they, not millions of parents, know what is best for their children; the courts have decided that they, not thousand of ministers know what is meant by "separation of church and state" (read simply—no state-established religion); the courts have decided that they, not the legislature of the states, know who can marry, who can kill an unborn baby, and what constitutes hate speech. We find ourselves doing things we should not do, because we might be sued if we don't; and we find ourselves not doing things we should do, because we might get sued if we do.

Some females say in an indignant manner, "How dare they tell us what we can or cannot do with our own bodies?" How shallow. They haven't even thought through what they are really saying. It is the baby's body that is mauled, mutilated, and killed in a grotesque death. The woman's body ... Well, the woman's body at most goes through a temporary but perfectly natural and routine process. How can a court, even the most inept court, not see the merits of the baby compared with a female being temporarily inconvenienced? Should she not have anticipated that possibility earlier? Do we not want to rejoice at a new life? I could easily classify abortion as premeditated murder, worthy of capital charges. A tiny life is helpless and at the mercy of a heartless adult.

How can anyone see the angelic face of a six-month-old baby, look into the sparkling eyes, examine the tiny fingers and toes, see the innocent and happy smile, and deny that this tiny life is the sacred work of God? No matter the skin color of the baby, it is depraved, cruel, and inhuman to murder this life, frequently in the name of convenience. Why a six month-old you ask. Well, that happens to be, at the time this is written, the exact age of a precious great-granddaughter of mine. How cruel and heartless can some humans be? We know that Hitler and some others that were cruel and heartless for inasmuch as you have killed one. Humans will be humans, sometimes less so. Therefore, I place only about 25 percent of the blame at the feet of the female. The other 75 percent belongs wholly to the Supreme Court, for this body is supposed to be the final man-made institution to ensure that justice, not convenience, prevails; and to keep the uncivilized element present in all of us in check, preventing barbaric acts. I can easily see how a minor could panic and make an abortion decision, but not so for an adult female. As previously stated, a court that can legalize abortion can legalize *anything*.

A TIME TO KILL AND A TIME TO LIFE

There has been and is a continuing debate among some people about when it is acceptable to kill a life. Is the time to kill at the first trimester, or is it the second, fourth or perhaps a tenth. The reason this debate rages on and that it can rage on proves that at any of those stages life already exists although as pointed out, it may not be the same as it was yesterday or will be tomorrow. So the debate can only be - is it okay to kill a life and if some consider it okay, then at what stage are you comfortable with murder.

It is queer how our legal system considers some acts that are the same different and their rationale. Where Jack Kevorkian can conduct an assisted suicide on the eighty-two year old terminally ill cancer patient and be tossed in jail, another person can kill a baby and walk free. In legal circles, damage awards for loss of life can be based on the earning potential of the individual. So on a strictly earning potential I would bet on the baby as having more earning potential than an eighty-two year old terminally ill cancer patient. This should serve to demonstrate clearly that the courts have no reason, no benchmarks, no anchor as a basis of operation - its background and experience, i.e. seat of pants(ies). No wisdom, no compassion. For a social agenda it willingly sacrifices its soul. Seems as if every time one turns around there is a group of people crying for "respect". It matters not to them that they have done little or nothing to respect. Apparently they consider in another "right" or "entitlement". I don't think so.

There are ways to work problems without doing injury to innocent white straight males (although it could be that a democrat does not believe there are any innocent white straight males). Doing harm to an innocent bystander in an attempt to resolve another problem is a criminal offense, yet the courts do that very criminal act on a routine basis. For example, the limited edition medical school admission policy. The courts have criminally violated the rights of white males (who usually have better scores) in order to insert minorities into a limited edition class. Would it not be more fair to simply ask the medical school to set up another chair? Sure it would, and no one is harmed in the process. But the courts have no adult supervision.

By the same token, well into my working career, I discovered that there are times when many lawyers need some adult supervision.

The executive office will not step in and say, "Okay, you have made your decision and now I'm making mine—get lost. Your ruling is clearly out of line with the Constitution, and I'm not enforcing your decision." The legislative branch of the federal government will not act to protect its prerogatives, instead allowing the courts to not only make a decision on so-called constitutional grounds, but to then direct their fix, clearly a legislative function. But the courts are well aware of exactly what they are doing, and they don't care because no one is willing to fight the battle to reel in courts that have run amuck. The courts also know a legislature might not implement what they have in mind (usually social engineering); or that a legislature might take years to act; or it might never act, and that in itself can be the just thing. Neither of the other two branches of government in this triumvirate have the moxie to stand up to the courts. Courts have the power to say something is constitutional or not, nothing more.

It is this arena where the courts have made themselves look ridiculous. In their quest to legislate what they want. It is impossible to avoid the noose of losing the logic used in one case, because it doesn't match the next case. Of course, that hasn't deterred the courts one whit. They just keep sailing along unsupervised and unchecked. The only constant is the consistent lean to the left. One of the reasons for this consistent left-wing bias is that the courts have totally lost perspective on the two key issues of rights and responsibilities. The courts have a hair-trigger on the "rights gun" and a use-all-your-strength trigger on the "responsibilities gun," when in fact both triggers should be equal and therefore fair.

On the surface it is easy to identify the extra-constitutional decisions. First they are lengthy and filled with rationale, which when read leaves one asking, "Now what the heck did that say?" On the other hand, a Supreme Court decision proclaiming that the Second Amendment says what it says is straight arrow. For this court fight, it was the complainers that had to conjure up the double-talk and outlandish rationale in their battle to destroy what little is left of the Constitution.

Even though a witness swears to tell the truth, the whole truth, and nothing but the truth, as soon as he is sworn in both lawyers set out, while the judge sits on his rear end, to confine the witness to only that element of the truth that is favorable to their cause. Taking elements out of context, preventing the "rest of the story" from being told, coaching witnesses, badgering and harassing witnesses, and so on, all are okay in the courtroom. Democrats would not subject a terrorist to this harsh questioning. A lawyer can even label a fed-up witness as a "hostile witness." Justice will be served when the witness or the judge labels a lawyer as a hostile lawyer, or better yet, challenges a lawyer for lying. Although I acknowledge the judges and lawyers of character, every one of them is caught up in a corrupt system. Corrupt, in this case, does not necessarily meaning money. The leading corrupt element without doubt is the corruption of the Constitution by "interpretation," but the list goes on and on. The system is a brotherhood of lawyers, all with the identical human weaknesses of that part of the population that are not members of the brotherhood. This brotherhood has no oversight, no audit, and can no more be expected to police itself than a doctor, university president, or garage mechanic. Oaths of high-sounding words are used primarily to justify their audit exempt status. All of them plead, as did the president who was elected in November 2008, that "we are a special case." Rubbish. It's about power and money, right down to the bitter end. If you don't believe it, read the rampant bribery records of judges and lawyers.

I was on the fringe of a class action lawsuit some years ago involving Delta Airlines. I refused to participate, but they kept sending me material. The last mailing I received was an accounting of the distribution of the award. As I recall, the guy who initiated the claim got about $7,000.00, but the lawyer got millions. I got zip. And so it was in the asbestos and tobacco class action lawsuits; and so it has been, is, and will be, so long as the legal system is a closed circuit. If one uses Aristotle's definition of justice, I see no reason why a judge can't simply be a person of character and not a lawyer. You do know who approves the lawyers' rewards for a class action case, don't you-- another lawyer, who just happens to be a judge. Do you not believe he will be generous to a brother?

Today's unprecedented level of murder, assault, rape, robbery, burglary, child abuse, child sex crimes, pornography, embezzlement, you name it, is almost wholly accounted for by court's and lawyers' permission. And the criminals are so bold, they don't even wait for the cover of darkness. Pick up your paper. It may be scattered over several sections, but paste them all together and you will be appalled at the daily total.

Given the rudderless and anchorless masses today, it is easy to connect that too many inexplicable jury decisions. Is it fair to reward a person with money, simply because another person or company has lots of insurance, or has money in the bank, or has "deep pockets"? No, but it is done every day. Not only is it wrong, but insult is added to injury by awarding outrageous sums in many, many cases, totally without merit, all because another person or company has money, and some idiotic jury seizes an opportunity to give it to another person. And the judge sits there on his rear end.

These same types of juries are the ones that let murderers and rapists off, and they are encouraged or enabled by lawyers and judges. A lawyer hired by a murderer or rapist to defend him is not obligated to cheat justice by getting the criminal off. In my opinion, he is only obligated to defend the person in the context of serving justice. Yet every day lawyers cheat the system just this way. Of course, it is not really the lawyer (or even the judge) that lets the murderer or rapist off. It is the jury that cheats justice, and that is a regular part of today's legal system. A California jury set a new low in this crazy thought process, and again the judge permitted it. In fact, he possibly aided the results. At a minimum, he allowed it.

Although neither the lawyers nor the judges would admit it, the judges are in chaos today. One man gets twenty-five years in a kickback scheme that nets him not one dime, while a high roller in a billion dollar scheme gets ten years and is allowed to keep most of the money. Another convicted on a fraud charge that nets him no money gets eighteen months, while an influence peddler in a long and massive bribery system is sentenced to only four years. Someone convicted of bribing a judge gets five years, a man gets thirty years for underage sex, while a woman gets off with a ruler stroke on the back of the hand. Don't even guess on the murder sentencing, as it could be anything from a plea bargain for a manslaughter sentence to life and beyond. Child rape may get probation or thirty years. These few examples are only a drop in the lake. And all of these are contingent on the case even making it to the court, and then contingent on getting a guilty verdict. We already know that one strong-willed person on a jury can shut down the whole process, or worse let a guilty man off. Just recently a judge in Vermont let a man off on probation for sexually abusing a four-year-old child. As previously stated, I believe a forty-five-year or older non-lawyer could hand out justice in most cases.

Today's criminal has more help these days in evading punishment than a dog has fleas: judges, the ACLU, a gazillion lawyers, all of Harvard's first year law school students, the NAACP, et cetera, while the victims have at most one overworked, understaffed district attorney. Needless to say, people just should not let themselves become victims. After all, as a victim you must in some way be at fault. My advice: keep a weapon handy.

About a week after the report of the guy out on probation even with eighteen arrests in three years, the newspaper reported on another guy arrested for burglary while out on bail for four prior burglaries. I'm probably not the smartest guy on the planet, but it would seem to me that if these guys were put away after the first, second, or even third event, there would be no fifth or eighteenth time! Do we waive the three strikes rule for a habitual criminal if the criminal is a member of a minority? Criminals repeat offenses because they know they can probably get away with it. Judging from local reports, most criminals are repeat offenders, and many of those are out on probation. Is it any wonder our crime rates are off the charts? The courts are releasing the criminals to roam free among the public. What do these judges expect these criminals to do when they are released? No, that is what you and I would think. The judge apparently thinks they are converted into instant angels.

Let's summarize:
1. Reverse discrimination is okay in many situations. (Ever figure out why they call it "reverse" discrimination?)
2. Political correctness is the number one rule. (See later for definition of political correctness.)
3. It's okay to shortchange the victim of a crime, but shortchange the criminal and all bets are off. Democrats couldn't care less about the poor victim, unless of course he is a minority, but they will go to the other side of rational to get the criminal off.
4. Preferential treatment for minorities is okay, regardless of the fact that your contract with the Feds says clearly you will not practice such evils. Aside from the contracts arm of the Feds, there is another arm, the Gestapo arm, that says, "Oh yes, you will." These particular people get preferential treatment in hiring, layoff s, promotions, et cetera. In one situation, a large company required that employees must pass a particular medical physical, with up to three retests before final disqualification. For one minority, the company ran

seven retests, and still was accused of racial discrimination and threatened with arbitration. Running seven retests on a straight white male could have been a firing offense.

5. Before the minority thing arrived on the scene, gerrymandering was outlawed by the Supreme Court, but now gerrymandering is not only permitted, but ordered by the courts.

6. History clearly says this nation was founded on a Christian foundation. But again, that was before this minority thing arrived on the scene. Today one person, I repeat, one person, can usually (with a court-sanctioned order) stop the wheels of the entire country. In the name of separation of church and state, the courts have made a mockery of our roots; and even have fostered an environment in which this Christian foundation can be openly mocked and ridiculed by the mass media, so-called artists, and even individual members of other religions or groups.

7. For all practical purposes, the mass media is a propaganda arm of the democrat party. Further, it makes no bones about it, because it knows you and I can do nothing about it except not watch.

8. The courts have politicized the First Amendment to the U.S. Constitution, as they have so many other things. It was recently revealed that when the Supreme Court was considering their decision on abortion, one of the ideas discussed was that it was a method to help control population growth. Hello, Constitution?

9. Courts render decisions which use the term unconstitutional. Actually, it is an outdated, even dead, term. The courts long ago left most of the Constitution in the dust. Even when it is referenced specifically, the court frequently puts its own twist on the reference section.

10. Five/four decisions. This is prima facie evidence that the legal system cries for reform. Any decision that close should not be made. This means that the pros and cons are so close, a single vote determines the direction of the entire notion. A 5/4 decision should be "no decision," as almost half the population feels disenfranchised. A better court would contain ten men, in which a split decision would result in no action. A 6/4 split would be the closest vote requiring action.

11. For all practical purposes, I believe ten educated men who are forty-five or older and are not law-school trained could make better decisions than any Supreme Court, as constituted in the past fifty years. Their decisions may not be technically in tune with the countless laws, precedents, et cetera, but they would be just.
12. The degree of political correctness required of the straight white male and Republican or Independent females is unbelievable, while a minority in any shape or form is not required to be politically correct.
13. Even political correctness is racially biased. What is considered politically correct depends greatly on your race, gender, or your degree of fame or infamy.
14. As originally constituted, there were three branches of government with "checks and balances." That worked pretty well for 175 or 180 years. Today that system has clearly failed. The lawyers and courts have made a mockery of the original government theory and practice. For it is the activist courts that have absolute power today, and, in fact, direct the affairs of the nation. The courts not only make decisions on the constitutionally of laws and situations, they give directions with their decisions. This is the function of a legislature or an executive, not a court. The courts have usurped this responsibility from the other two branches of government, and the cowardly people in the other legislature and executive branches have failed to do anything more than recognize that they have been had. Sure, the courts have federal marshals, but the president has the entire military and Congress holds the purse strings. Use of those two powerful cudgels would bring the courts to heel immediately.

When it suits their purposes, the democrats like to throw out the line, "We are a nation of laws." The fact is, we are supposed to be and sometimes are, but a democrat or the courts will trample any law that gets in the way of their agenda. They claim a right to appeal to a "higher law." This "higher law," please note, applies only to liberal or politically correct issues. Sometimes, though, the courts or a democrat will just claim that the law has not been correctly interpreted or whatever. Anything to avoid the law as has been applied. Conservatives or dependents need not apply.

A classic example can be found in the laws that apply to murder, probably the ultimate crime. There is no statute of limitations for murder. The law can reach back fifty years or more, but three things it cannot do: (1) it cannot punish a dead man, (2) it cannot punish the dead man's relatives, and (3) it cannot punish the society or culture of a time past. Yet that is exactly what the courts have done for carefully selected peoples in this post-World War II society (and perhaps even before). What the courts have done in this area is not based on law, it is not based on equal justice, it is not based on the Constitution. One may ask, if it is not based on one of these three foundations, then what is it based on and why. The answer to that question is simple. These irrational decisions are based on the personal whims of the court members or the individual judge. As to why, the answer to that part of the question is simply to drive society to remake itself in line with the courts' vision of what society should be. But what it amounts to is courtroom gerrymandering, and it is absolutely unconstitutional. It also denies equal protection and justice to one or more citizens every time such a decision is reached.

JUSTICE DENIED

In the fall of 2009, a former county circuit judge went on trial for a number of charges involving young men who were themselves charged with various crimes. He was originally indicted on 103 counts of sexual abuse, sodomy, second-degree assault, extortion, kidnapping, and ethics charges. When faced with these charges, he resigned his judgeship in 2007. Apparently the deal with this judge and the young men was that the men would go free in exchange for granting him his desires. Fifteen young men testified that they did so.

I previously stated that our court system long ago lost its stature as a justice system, and is an empty, hollow legal system. Aside from the men's verbal testimony, a forensic expert testified that he found semen from two of the witnesses on the judge's office carpet. Please follow this legal system's version of justice.

- 103 court indictments

- The number of indictments was reduced by 4/5 (eighty-two) before the case went to the jury. Some were dropped by the prosecutor, and extortion, kidnapping, and other charges were thrown out by the judge. T at left twenty-one charges for the jury to consider.
- The jury found the former judge not guilty on seven charges.
- The presiding judge dismissed the remaining fourteen charges.

The presiding judge in this case and the prosecutor are not known, and the composition of the jury is not known. However, one is reminded of a case in California some years ago where a guy was found not guilty in a double murder—regardless of the evidence. Many folk credited the man's lawyer with getting him off the hook, but actually it was the jury that let him off. In this case, I suspect the same. No matter the charges and no matter the evidence, this jury was not going to convict this guy. The presiding judge quickly dispensed with the remaining charges against his brother lawyer and judge. Again, a local case, but the question begs to be asked. How many times is this repeated across the country each day? Justice denied in a broken and failed system.

Even as the failure of our justice system is chronicled, Senate democrats voted down a bill that would have made it clear that prisoner-of-war detainees held at off -shore facilities would be tried in a military court. T us there remains a possibility that they could be brought to this country and thrown into the court system's morass here. The question jumps out at one. What are the democrats thinking when they pull off something this dumb?

- We know liberals hate the military with a passion, and they know the military believes it is their right and their responsibility to try foreign prisoners captured by the U.S. military on foreign soil. The liberals want to just give the military a big middle finger to show their hatred.
- Could it be that the democrats just want to toss these people into what they know will be a bonanza for their friends, the trial lawyers and judges, as a political reward?
- Could it be that the democrats just want to delay the possibility of any justice in a system known for its capacity to drag on for five, ten, fifteen, or even twenty years?

- Or could it be they just want to see these people go unpunished?

Let us make sure everyone understands: these people were actively engaged in attempting to kill Americans, or certainly aiding in that attempt. What possible motive could a legal citizen of the U.S. have in aiding their release or mitigating their punishment, unless they are sympathetic to their cause?

MORE ON THE SUBJECT OF COURTS AND JUDGES

The supreme arbiter of justice is itself a victim of the imbalance between individual rights and individual responsibilities. The court has lost all sense of justice in their wanton desire to bestow rights on minorities, criminals, causes, especially left wing causes, and some single purpose cause by one vocal individual. They do this with total disregard to their responsibilities, the rights of society to be protected from the criminals, the rights of the majority and the common good. They have now permitted the judicial system to be used and abused by anyone that has the money to buy a lawyer or the connections to enlist the ALCU in their "cause". All this could be an exercise in "feel good", "ego building" and "power". It must be very satisfying to any and all judges to have the entire country at your door pleading for you to share your great wisdom with them. For whatever the ruling and your (sometimes) bizarre basis for ruling you will be idolized by the winner and the loser, well they are just "sour grapes" or " sore losers". One can easily see how any judge or even an ordinary man would find this process very exhilarating and could easily begin to think of themselves and their brethren as a cut above the ordinary citizen. A feeling of superiority could set in, especially when one knows it is a lifetime job with all the trimming and more. In fact the nation's judges represent a cross section of our society. Some of them are drunks, some of them are guilty of taking bribes, some of them are adulterers, some of them sit in judgment of situations where they have a self interest, some of them are bigots with all the biases of the society of which they are part, yet all of them wear a cloak of royalty. We do have one plus however, when they enter a room we do not have to bow; we only have to stand. You are not required to stand for the nation's anthem, however. Does that translate to contempt of nation; yes, I believe it does.

The abuse of the constitution is not a recent issue however. If started almost as soon as the country was founded with what was perceived then as a good thing, and perhaps it was. A "broad" interpretation of the constitution began over 200 years ago. Regardless of the good or bad of these early years, it is over all bad for it has led directly to today's abuse of the constitution by a light headed court. As I read the constitution it appears that the framers feared most the executive and legislative branches and thus the safe-guards. I believe that the thought of judicial abuse never seriously crossed their minds. After all when one is selected to sit in judgment why would the framers think a person selected for such a calling would be the very person that the entire country would one day live in fear of becoming a dictator to the very citizens it was set up to protect. Obviously, they did not foresee today's judges or the constitution drafters would have added some choice words aimed at the courts and/or judges. Since the courts have strayed so far outside the constitution for their pronouncements the best American citizen can pray for today is something that has been lost in the melee-justice.

To put the rights and responsibilities imbalance in focus in this country one has only to consider one question: how many times have you read or heard of the ACLU initiating a lawsuit on behalf of someone using the term responsibilities (not rights). Any responsibility noted is laid at the feet of the company or person being sued; never the plaintiff. The truth is that untold millions have been unjustly stolen from individuals and/or companies because the lawyer (permitted by the courts) will acknowledge no responsibility on part of their client. The courts (judges) have allowed even the hint of a possibility of responsibly on the part of a defendant company to carry the day while an undeniable responsibility on the part of the plaintiff is brushed aside. This imbalance is not only wrong it is unjust. Just as class action lawsuits are unjust.

Two branches of the Federal government concern me for they can lead us down the wrong path or as a minimum the second, third or fourth best path. But they have some limitations on their power such as term limits.

Also Congress is a 500 plus body and it has been shown that it is difficult to "herd cats". On the other hand, the Supreme Court I panic over, for it has none of the checks that the executive and legislative branches have. There are no term limits and there is no appeal. Five (5) votes from people mostly voting their own passions form a dictatorship of the entire country. That the executive and legislative branches have allowed this cancer on our country is a sign of weakness of will, resolve and character that is literally tearing our once great country into shreds.

How many times have we seen it – a judge imposes an edict which one of the lawyers doesn't like. What happens; why he just goes next door to a judge he has figured out over time that will give him an edict that he likes. And, Shazam, the judge next door in a heartbeat grants him his wishes. Now one of those judges is wrong. This scene is played out across this country every day, every day. The masses are unaware of this because only once in a while does the public get informed via the papers or television. Justice, wherefore art thou?

To justify their varying decisions the lawyers/judges simply say that every case is different and therefore there are different sentences for what may appear to be the same violation of the law. That is their position and they stand on it and most folks buy in just as big as when Uncle Walter said "and that's the way it is…." Please don't.

The decisions are different because they have essentially trashed the constitution and each judge is flying by the seat of his pants or panties; that is in the words of Sotomayer, based on their individual "background and experience". THAT is why the decisions are so wildly different. It is my opinion that the actual cases that may merit, due to some unique circumstance, special sentencing only plays a minor role in the total.

The public is already aware of the predisposition of some judges to give special (and therefore unequal) consideration to big money, big names and brothers in the law. With little or no oversight these little kingdoms operate all over the nation in a vacuum mostly shielded from supervision and correction. To repeat what is already clear; today's courts are the single largest violator of the United States constitution in the country. In recent years we have seen one of these judges in a hick state perhaps with an axe to grind of his own, doesn't just rule on the constitutionality of an issue but to aggressively issue a sweeping order of immediate action. Has he overstepped his authority. In my opinion he has already done that for he has trespassed on a duty assigned to the Congress. But with little or no supervision he can carry the day once more in violation of the constitution. Readers think about this for a little. This is not Congress acting on behalf of the people, this is not even the Supreme Court, this is a single guy acting out his own prejudices with all of force of a king in a little kingdom. These things cry out for remedial action. If the courts fail to manage their own house then the other two branches of the central government are responsible to do that.

LACK OF CRIMINAL RESPONSIBILITY

Right in step with the Supreme Court some elements in our society are obsessed with the rights of a criminal, sometimes a person they don't even know and have never heard of except through reports of the media regarding the person's criminal activity. For some queer reason this element of the population identifies with this criminal to the extent that they are sympathetic to the guy and in some cases are willing to attempt to intervene in the court system on this person's behalf. There are even cases where someone has so identified with the criminal they will marry the person even where he may have no chance of a release from prison. They are willing to write letters, sign petitions on his behalf and even participate in all night vigils. Sound irrational. These people are blind to the responsibilities of the criminal to obey the laws and apparently have no interest in holding him accountable for his crimes.

Wait we're not finished with this topic. The above situations we see and/ or hear routinely from the media. However, how many times have you seen/heard this segment of the population cry out on behalf of the victim. Other than family members; you have probably never heard it. It is almost as if the victim is responsible to stay out of the criminals' path because the criminal has a right to be where he was. The thinking of this segment of the population is so distorted that, no matter how heinous the crime he becomes a victim and the victim or victims family are the bad guys for prosecuting this person.

Although laws are on the books for the sole purpose to prevent criminal activities just stating the obvious is not enough. There must be an accounting, otherwise the criminal is free to go his own way over and over again and again. The law can and does state thou shall not kill or rape or steal or whatever all it wants over and over again but without the <u>direct punishment</u> element it is of no effect. So why do people that would never take up a victims cause for justice take up the cause of the criminal when he is the lawbreaker. Why do the courts who are supposed to see justice done, appear to do loop-de-loops is to get the criminal off the charge(s).

Want to hear a good one reported by the locally distributed newspaper: Seems as if this lawyer was charged with drunk driving according to the testimony of six (6) officers. In court the judge let him off because the officer that filled out the ticket signed the ticket but did not put his title on the ticket. I say unbelievable, crazy, unjust; ridiculous - all this and more.

It appears that to many, including the courts, there are few or no responsibilities on the part of the criminal. However, they give the criminal every conceivable right including the "right" to a lawyer that may trash justice over and over in an attempt to get his guy off the hook. The criminal is responsible for all his crimes. The fact is that some lawyer, some jury or some judge may let him off the hook. In my view he's still responsible for his crimes. Thank goodness that when that actually happened in a murder trial in California another judge and another jury did hold the criminal responsible even if the responsibility was only of a financial nature. A little punishment is better than no punishment. Unfortunately, this scenario is not the normal where a person that commits a crime is let off by some lawyer, jury or judge.

Let's look at the twisted conduct of the courts on the issue of responsibility. If an individual claims he is suffering from some disease that may or may not have been the result of his vocation (and sometimes that is impossible to prove either way, it may be a naturally occurring disease) he is given the benefit of the doubt. The data clearly show there is an increasing frequency rate of cancer with increasing age. Many chemicals in use in the home or workshop are carcinogenic. Some people smoke or listen to loud music. Nevertheless should the man allege his disease is due to his employer the employer then is charged with full responsibility. If his employer of 30 years went out of business any work for another similar company for only a few months or year that employer is then yoked with full responsibility for this man. On the other hand no matter what an individual has done or not done only rarely is he ever held responsible. In fact, I cannot recall a single one where an individual was held responsible for his own conduct. Regardless of what the cigarette companies did or did not do it was known at least 70 years ago that habitual smoking was dangerous to one's health. Even where a guy is hurt as a result of his own negligence someone else is frequently held liable. Things such as these, although proven in isolated cases, become automatics to certain others. The rule is one of presumed guilt. If X and Y are given Z is assumed. I don't buy it. I want every case proven. This approach will cut down on many awards. Take the allegations of second hand smoke. I don't buy that for one second. My sibling and I and my Cousins all grew up in an environment where all the men smoked heavily. Yet not a single one of us developed lung cancer except one sister and she and her husband were heavy smokers.

HATE CRIMES

In today's court environment of social engineering directed to molding the great American Society into something that was never intended or envisioned consider this enormous anomaly. Should one burn a cross, the fed's come after you as that has been deemed a "hate crime" and they put you in the pokey. However, should one burn the American flag, well the court has ruled that burning to be a freedom of expression act protected by the freedom of speech article of the constitution. Do you see the twisted and shallow reasoning. If burning a cross is a "hate crime" then burning the American flag is an even greater "hate crime" in addition to being an act of treason, and that twist of reason is exactly what happens when the courts leave the constitution in the dust and trust to their own "experience and background."

For the liberal, before you can even get started on your favorite rebuttal allow me to cut you off at the knees. Burning of the American flag in the town square by an angry mob or an angry individual is clearly an act of hate and in no way I can be compared with the disposition of a worn and torn but loved flag in the privacy of a man's backyard. The only way a court could get something like that wrong is to have a predisposition to the outcome before the game even starts. Think about this for a few minutes. Although I am unable to find a definition of a hate crime in the dictionary do you really want to trust some judge to rule that some act is a hate crime or not. We have already seen that if one does not like a given pronouncement at a given time and place, he can go next door or next town or next county and get a different ruling. In today's court environment that is not something in which I would have the slightest confidence. Since the constitution has largely been trashed by the courts and they have gone off into their own "experience and background" we know there are infinite shades of those commodities and therefore the possibility of infinite shades of rulings. Deliver us from such a court environment. Have you ever seen a definition of "hate crime". No, and it is not likely you will, for at that stage it would backlash on the liberals who today are exempt from "hate crimes."

TECHNICALITIES IN PERSPECTIVE

Yes, we have all seen or heard of the judge in a heartbeat throw out a case on the basis that the accused may have been denied equal protection under the law or the evidence may not have been obtained in exact accord with established procedures or some such technicality. There is, I believe a better, a much better way. Were I a sitting judge presented with such a possibility I was simply say; "Yes, I can see your point and there may be a course for action there which can be addressed at the proper time and place. In the meantime this trial is a matter of your indictment and charges for rape, assault, robbery and murder. There may be a question of how the evidence was obtained, however the validity of the evidence and its importance to rendering this a fair trial requires that this evidence be admissible. As earlier indicated you have the option to obtain redress at another time and place. Otherwise it appears that the court is searching for ways to dismiss or throw out evidence and frequently I believe they are.

THE LAWYER WINS AGAIN

In a legal action that I know of, a client asked a lawyer to sue another person for money and two or three perceived grievances. I have no way of knowing what the lawyer expected the outcome to be but his client certainly did not foresee the outcome. The client not only had no relief from the perceived grievances, he was told to pay for things that he had never before paid for plus he was told to pay a large lawyer fee. I venture to say the client should never have asked a lawyer to file suit because even to a novice the outcome, especially on the perceived grievance was fairly obvious. And if the client persisted the lawyer who surely knew better should have refused the case, by advising his client you can't win this one." However, I suspect the lawyer had his eye more on his prize than his clients' prize for should his client win or lose HE was sure to win. He was in a win, lose or tie, still going to collect his large fee. Could one call that an abuse of the legal system- why ,yes one could.

LAWYERS

Lawyers contribute nothing to the wealth of the nation. Although many of them are wealthy far beyond the wildest dreams of the average American citizen, they are overhead cost to the nation. They make nothing of value; although they may (or may not) be of dubious service to an individual, company or agency that has the money to hire them. They are in many cases contract labor for which you have no guarantee of anything. They are a huge drag on the economy of the nation and an impediment to economic growth. In the social sector they are far more successful at limiting the freedoms as defined by the constitution of the majority of America citizens than they are at protecting these freedoms. With sympathetic judges they are however, renown for securing some special, if questionable, privilege to a person or a few people with a pet cause or an axe to grind. In fact it appears that many lawyers and judges enjoy the role of cheating justice in order to win a "pet cause" case with little or no merits but an in-your-face to the majority of American citizens. Can they in any stretch of the imagination really believe that this is for the good of or in the will of the majority of Americans. I believe not; rather it is to further their own goal of remaking the country into their own image and, of course, increasing their wealth. Although these one act plays are frequently portrayed as securing some right for a single individual more often than not it is the denial of some right to everyone else in the country. So it is not about an individuals rights - it is his option that he wants to choose at the expense of others. What we have is a society where the lawyers and the courts have chipped away at the rights of the majority and at the clear words of the constitution to the point the country is not the country of the founders and the laws and the constitution distorted to the point there is legal chaos in the land and fairness and justice have been sacrificed in the name of legal. In a radical left administration the old "Justice" Department must be renamed the "Legal" Department and even then one must tack on "for selected ones".

AMENDMENT XXVIII TO THE UNITED STATES CONSTITUTION

Is it too late to put Pandora back in her box; perhaps, but it is not too late to stop the bleeding. The citizen should demand a constitutional amendment that will impose some basic controls on the Supreme Court such as constitutional framers would have put in place had they envisioned today's court abuse. There are specific controls on the other two branches of the central government because the framers saw the potential for abuse. In fact, one prominent framer of the constitution, Thomas Jefferson, did warn of the possibility of abuse by the courts – exactly as has happened in today's courts. He was a prophet in his own time. Such an amendment would have to be carefully crafted to allow the court freedom to do its job while still remaining within the words of the constitution. There must be a method of control by direct intervention when the court strays off into social engineering and legislative functions. It may be too much to hope for but perhaps there could be a process to roll back the courts more obvious abuses and return the judicial branch to a justice system rather than a legal system.

BEARING THE UNBEARABLE

GM going bankrupt, circa 1959. It would never happen, impossible, unthinkable. Fast forward fifty years, to 2009. It is not only possible, but it actually happened. What happened in the intervening fifty years? (Not listed in order of impact severity.)

1. GM management grossly underestimated the foreign threat and the domestic market needs.
2. GM management transitioned from a technocrat to a bean counter.
3. GM, along with the rest of the country, was hijacked into social engineering of workforce.
4. GM abrogated its responsibility and allowed unions to basically take over many management decisions.
5. GM makes series of incredibility bad decisions concerning its product lines, e.g., Vega.
6. GM lost an edge it had enjoyed most of its corporate life in design and styling.
7. American public abandons GM in droves. (Not that they didn't have legitimate causes to be disgusted with GM.)
8. A fifty-year decline in moral, ethical, and spiritual values
9. In the last thirty years, a flood of foreigners that has totally changed the character of this once great country, including GM

Last fall, when the report of General Motors being in extremis and the word bankruptcy was used, I was disbelieving, and then became very upset. For a product of the Great Depression, the well-being of GM was almost synonymous with the well-being of our country. In fact, some may remember well Charlie Wilson's famous words (and the mockery of some in the media).

After six months or so of hard hand wringing, however, a couple of things have risen to the surface. First, Wilson's words really are still true. Think about it. Second, General Motors as Charlie Wilson knew it no longer exists, and the United States of America as I knew it no longer exists. One could write a book or two on either demise. The demise of either was impossible fifty years ago. Today the impossible has come to pass, and not only has it become a reality, but it came to pass from within. The U.S. did not fall to the Nazis, nor to the communists, nor to any external enemy. Like Rome, the demise came from internal rot and some of the identical problems.

As part of a bankruptcy scheme, GM formulated several cost-cutting measures. One of these was elimination of the Pontiac. One may recall GM eliminated the Oldsmobile a few years back. In the 1940s, 1950s, and 1960s, these were General Motor icons. Eight of the first ten cars I owned were Pontiacs. Even though I was very disturbed about the announced elimination of the Pontiac, the announcement was only for the funeral.

GM had killed the Pontiac long ago. It was only a delayed burial. There are probably more factors contributing to the death of General Motors than most are aware of. However, the three that are most prominent are (1) turning over the management of the company to the bean counters; (2) management yielding part of its responsibilities to the labor unions; and (3) a total loss of styling and, in many instances, half-baked engineering. One cannot take one of the largest and most successful companies in the world into bankruptcy except through incompetence in management.

I am reminded that in the middle of the twentieth century, General Motors was king of the styling hill. After the loss of Harley Earl, it began to slip, a slip that has not been halted to this day. Need one call attention to the ridiculous "star war" Cadillac? With the styling division already in deep yogurt several years ago, I was surprised to read in the locally distributed paper that a new head of the styling division had been named. I silently said, "Thank goodness," until the rest of the article reported that the new styling chief had previously headed the refrigerator division, to which there was a silent groan of "Oh, my goodness." Is there anyone on the planet that can make a connection between refrigerator styling and car styling?

Hold on, we are not finished with this subject yet. Beyond the company management, gigantic outside forces have complicated everything at a minimum. At the worst, they put a stop to anything, including the very life of a business. The culprits in this fandango are the EPA, the Department of Labor, unions, lawyers, courts, countless laws and rules and regulations by countless government agencies, et cetera.

Some of you may have heard of Lockheed's famous Skunk Works, a small group of competent engineers who were capable of building, from scratch, highly technical products in an unbelievably short time for the military. It is my opinion that such an operation could not exist in the U.S. today; and if it could, it would never get anything done. Factor in the heavyweights just noted with an unstable environment, and one has a recipe for disaster. Laws, courts, the population, even the price of gasoline are in a continuing state of flux, which fosters lack of confidence and makes for unreliable decision making.

A SELF RELIANT PEOPLE

In the past 50 years we have transitioned from a mostly self reliant nation to a mostly government reliant nation. Look around, smell it, if you're not careful you will step in it if you so much as move a muscle. Ironically, even though John Kennedy's speech writer dreamed up a clever line of "ask not….", it was in his administration that the seed of "government reliant" fell on fertile ground. Johnson fertilized it with plenty of horse manure and every president since then has done his share or more to play Santa. All evidentially forget that Santa only comes once per year, not three times a day, every day. In the process of playing Santa he and others have transitioned a nation of industrious adult men and women into a society of "what's in it for me", "what can I get from the government", "everybody is doing it, why shouldn't I get some freebies", etc. etc. Thus the communist mentality of "why should I bust my butt for other people's benefit" has taken over, few are willing to carry the load and thus the industrial revolution is quietly murdered.

Hoards of people are at the government door asking for money to pay their livelihood:

If one wants to operate a radio broadcasting system that broadcasts propaganda to the public and is unable to make it pay for itself they want public money to support them.

If one wants to operate an artsy association that is unable to make it pay for itself they want government money to pay for their fantasies.

If one wants to operate a school they want even more government money for their "new math" or "new reading" or "revised history", or other off the wall experiments.

If one is a college professor looking to increase his income he wants a government grant to study the television watching habits of a cockroach.

If one has a big city or big state that has spent itself into a hopeless debt he wants government bailout bucks.

If one has a large company or bank or whatever and has accumulated debt to the point he can never repay it he wants government (public) money to save him.

The list is endless. About the only group of people in the country that does not have his hand out for government money is what is left of the class of people that was at one time called the blue collar worker. Now given today's environment; that may be a politically incorrect term. However in the late great United States these were the backbone of the country. They were not individual heroes, but they were steady, dedicated, honest, hard working people that had a family to take care of and a job to do every day and they did both. They were not late for work, they were not absent from work; they were on the job day in and day out. The jobs these people had was not flipping hamburgers, making sandwiches or salads; these people were building something that had value to it, lasting value. It could be an iron, a refrigerator, a washing machine, a piece of furniture, clothing, shoes, automobiles or trucks, lawn mowers, rakes, shovels, lumber, tires or 1000 other products for a million buyers. Regardless of how the New York liberals looked down their nose at these people their value to the country was infinitely more than the liberal maker of nothing except trouble. Actually the liberal media usually found in the northeast part of the country, except possibly some amusement or entertainment value (or just killing time) are as zero value to the wealth of the nation. They could be of some value if they fully informed the public on issues such that the public was educated to the degree they could make intelligent decisions based on merits of the pro's and con's. Of course, the typical New York media motor mouth apparently believes that the American masses do not have the intellect to make good decisions so they feel obligated to slant the news in the direction they want the masses to vote. And in fact it does work for them –the election of November 2008 is a prime example of their efforts. They withheld all the negative information concerning their boy while only showing him in peak form, reading from cue cards in a staged scenario. Hitler and Goebbels would be proud of them.

THE NATIONAL WORK ETHIC

When I was growing up and become an adult, the Social Security System was almost exactly my age; it was growing up and for a few, beginning to mature. In that day so long ago the working class was everybody. There may have been differences in jobs and pay but I can hardly remember a single soul that was retired or unemployed. People worked because they had to eat, pay rent (although it may be just $5.00), have some clothing etc. There was no welfare class because other than a very few old people at the county home there was no welfare. There was available to a few people something called commodities. These were foodstuffs but certainly not something one could live off of. Generally the children also worked, especially those living on the farms which at that time was probably half the population. In town young boys sometimes delivered papers, groceries, medicines for drug stores, and other odd jobs like mowing lawns. In these days lawns were mowed with an old fashion lawnmower. The kid not only had to push the mower to make it go forward he also had a push it to make the cutting blade turn. No power mower back then. For those not old enough to remember this was a time when a lady could phone her grocery list into the grocer; he had people collect and package it and a delivery boy delivered it to her kitchen counter. The lady never left the house. As stated almost 100% of the population that was not handicapped or disabled in some way worked.

In my first year of high school (9th grade) the football coach got the players summer jobs at a local sawmill supposedly to toughen them up for football season. At that time, 1947 the hourly rate for a grown man was 75¢ an hour. Most of the men were farmers that worked at the mill during the day and at 4:00 PM headed back to the farm as quickly as they could to finish up all the farm chores of the day. I guarantee you no one ever had to rock these guys to sleep at night. When they laid their bodies out on their bed I'm sure that they were sound asleep in seconds. As for this guy, believe me he wanted to get tough, to get in shape for football season but he was actually far more interested in making a grown man's wages. It was far better than delivering papers or groceries or cutting grass. It was good money for a kid who needed money for clothes, bicycles and spending money. And that is how I came to pay my first few dollars into the Social Security System. I was 15 years old. I paid into this System until I was 68 years old.

My mother was one of the workers of the day. Although she never worked outside the home until my dad passed away and out of necessity she had to seek employment outside the home. Mom was a housewife and mother and in those days that was a fulltime job requiring skill and talent. She did it all, first up in the morning and the last to bed at night. With eight children to raise there was no time for tea and crumpets with the neighbors. She cooked three hot meals a day almost every day. For breakfast there was always her "from scratch" biscuits, eggs, grits and sausage, bacon or ham. On special days it was just biscuits, tomato gravy and sausage, bacon or ham. We lived only 1/2 block from the school so all the school age children came home to another hot meal at noon. After school, not always but most days there were hot cookies (homemade of course) when we all hit the door. In the evening we had another hot meal.

Dad was a great scrounger when he was not on the road. From early spring until the middle of September when the sand pears came in he bargained with the local farmers for dew berries, huckleberries, cantaloupes, cucumbers, eggplant, squash, peaches, plums, peas, beans, pecans, corn, tomatoes, apples, watermelons, okra, figs, potatoes, strawberries and pears. In the winter he came home with the farmers results of their slaughtering hogs and cattle for their own table. All of this bounty of the countryside had to be canned in preparation for feeding the family during the fall, winter and spring until another farming season started. Although dad and all the "older" children were pressed into service Mom was in charge of the canning operation. Usually the process started out on the front screen porch with bushels of corn, beans, peaches or whatever. The corn had to be shucked and de-silked, beans said to be shelled, peaches had to be peeled, each product in its turn. Then the cooking, preparation of the jars and lids, filling the jars, tightening the cap on the piping hot jars, waiting for the lids to pop and finally storage in the pantry up off the kitchen. It was serious and hard work. But at the end of canning season, September, one could step into the pantry and from floor to ceiling one would find shining jars containing the fruits of the farms and of our labors. At that time the pantry was chock full. During the winter the pantry was gradually drained of its treasure like a leaking bucket. By the end of spring it was essentially empty and the cycle would start over again.

Mom washed all our clothes with a semi-automatic washer and all had to be hung out each time on a multi-stranded clothes line I had rigged. She ironed every piece (until the girls got old enough to iron) to keep her children neat and clean even if the fabrics were thin. Boys did not iron in those days. They had other chores, cutting the grass, raking the yard, cutting wood for three fireplaces, wood and coal for fires, building fires and keeping them going, taking out ashes, and sometimes a part time job. Truthful, to this day I have never learned to iron or vacuum. Mom kept the house as well as she could with a host of her own kids and sometimes the neighbors kids running in and out. She took care to clip our nails and sometimes even help with homework.

Mom was a God fearing woman with a deep belief in her Lord. She read scripture to us, gave us lessons in morals and conduct; etiquette and sent us to Sunday school and church every Sunday. She rarely went because there seemed to be a little one around. She made it unnecessary for any of us to have to ask "Who am I?" or "Why am I here?" and those type of questions. Thanks Mom!

Mom could knit, quilt, crochet and sew. She was an expert seamstress making many of the girls' school clothing from patterns purchased at the local stores, all the while listening too " Stella Dallas" or other programs on the radio. As the girls got older and the need for evening gowns became a reality she made those also. She was so talented and making evening gowns a neighbor's daughter attending Ole Miss at the time asked her to make her evening gown for a contest at school. Mom made her gown and the girl won the competition. Where she found time for all this I do not know but she "got'er done". She did all this beautiful work on an old foot powered New Home sewing machine. Those of us still down here miss you, Mom.

THE COMPANY STORE

The late Tennessee Ernie Ford was a great and popular singer and in one of his songs he, it is deep rich voice, mentioned "the company store". Probably many adults and almost all young people have no idea what "the company store" was. For one thing they long ago disappeared from the American landscape. A TEF fan would recall immediately a line in the song that goes something like this –"St. Peter, don't you call me, I can't go; I owe my soul to the company store." There was a company store in the village of my birth. The reason there was a company store there was that during World War Two there was a huge demand for lumber and with an almost unlimited supply of hardwoods and pines locally, there was a good size sawmill on the north edge of the village. The people that owned the saw mill also owned the company store. Each week when the mill hands got paid they got paid in coupons such as those one got at the movie theatre. Each coupon had its' value printed on it: –5¢, 10¢, 25¢ etc. This was a nice arrangement for the owner of the saw mill and the company store for the coupons were good only at the company store. The mill employees had to purchase all of their needs at the company store using the mill issued coupons. They were not valid at any other store. Now if one needed something the store did not stock he can go in and try to convince a clerk that he needed something the company store did not stock. Simply wanting another brand of an item was not good enough. If successful he could trade coupons in for real money and then go to another store in the next town, which was about 5 miles away, and purchase the item(s). Neat, huh? At least it was for the owners. Of course the saw mill and the company store are long gone; but one of the descendants of the owners lives locally even today. I tell this little tale to remind people that it has not been too long ago that there was a huge working class of people that scratched out a living by hard work. I knew these people and while they may have had very little money they earned their way. They were not wards of the government. They were honest, respectable and good people.

And before you liberals ask; they were white and black and that does not change the opinion I hold of them – they were good people. Yes, I am well aware that was a different day and a different time. But it was also a better day and a better time. There were many low income, even poor people, but very few trashy people.

THE LAST MILL

How bad is it. The great manufacturing centers of the mid-west and northeast, as such, disappeared to overseas long ago. In Reading, Pennsylvania dozens of buildings that once made up a thriving mill town now house "outlet stores". These outlets are not selling goods made in the U.S.A. These buildings were long ago gutted of their manufacturing machinery and that equipment shipped overseas where it now provides jobs for citizens of another country and wealth for that nation.

More recently and on a much smaller scale, for it was the last mill, this scene was re-enacted in a tiny community in Clarke County, Mississippi: Stonewall. A small clothing mill was founded there in 1890. The mill made mostly denim products and during World War II it manufactured military uniforms. During its' peak the mill probably never employed more than 500 people, but in the community of less than 2000 it was a critical community asset. A few years back the locally distributed newspaper reported its death. The mill was gutted and the machinery shipped to Asia where it was reassembled to make things to sell to Americans. At its death I believe the paper indicated the mill employed 235 people. The significance of this event was and is that from the backwaters of Mississippi from a tiny community, a small clothing mill, the last mill in the county, is all that some unthinking bean counter could find left to ship overseas.

There are those among us that buy foreign cars and at least the United States does still have an automobile/truck manufacturing capability. Even that, however, is shrinking due to the American citizens buying foreign cars. Even employees of the American companies buy foreign cars. If asked about their foreign car, many people will respond with something like "why this car is made here in the United States". That may be true and that may ease the pain to our economy; however it misses at least two critical factors necessary for the continued success of any business venture. These people haven't thought about it or have overlooked it; but the profit from the sale of these vehicles goes overseas and the technological improvements necessary to make manufacturing and design advances all go overseas with these profits. Thus even purchasing a foreign car made in this country only delays a greater pain that is certain to come.

When the current administration speaks of creating jobs I do not believe they have even a clue what they're doing. This country does not need another minimum wage job; it needs manufacturing jobs, it needs those jobs we have been shipping overseas the last 40 years - and that, citizens, doesn't happen overnight. To even begin to bring these jobs back takes capital, lots of it, planning, ingenuity, creativity, cooperative labor and cooperative and helpful federal government. Of all of the necessities to accomplish this, I am most skeptical of the latter; after all, someone may have to tell that EPA or this EEO or the AB CD to sit down and shut up. In many situations, and this could be one, the best thing the federal government could do is simply to get the hell out of the way.

Adding another staffer for MO or another lawyer for the legal department will not correct the problem. Drinking one's own bath water never does. If fact, after observing the current administration for two years I am convinced that their brain tissue is so hardened around a victim mentality it could not in another 150 years think in the terms necessary to make our country wealthy once again. They are so warped mentally they cannot think straight in the box or out of the box.

PART II

MEDIA PROPAGANDA

Walter Cronkite died in 2009 at ninety-two years of age. Among the many analyses of his life and times, an adoring media guy opined that it was only after his retirement that Cronkite became a liberal. I say, that is untrue. He anchored a news program for about twenty years, and during that times I referred to him as Uncle Walter (as in Uncle Joe Stalin), for it was obvious he was managing the news so he could present a story exactly as he wanted it slanted. The old Soviet state-controlled paper of the Cold War, *Pravda*, could not have done a better job. To me, and probably to many others, it was so obvious that Cronkite played loose with the truth. I wrote a letter to the editor of *Time* or *Newsweek* (don't remember which) in which I referred to him as Uncle Walter. Cronkite appeared to think he knew what was best for us, and therefore he steered the news in that direction. That he was a liberal was beyond question.

But please, please, don't just take the word of this ole southern boy. Let others prove it. To a man the *New York Times*' columnists have heaped praise and adoration on Cronkite since his passing. One doesn't get that treatment from these know-it-alls unless he is a fellow traveler. But there is further proof provided by others that Cronkite was a liberal from the get-go. The mass media have idolized him almost to the point of sainthood. They have even said that when Cronkite said, "And that's the way it is," well, by golly, you could believe to the bottom of your heart (if not your brain) that that's the way it was! Once again, one does not get that loving treatment unless one is a dedicated liberal. No conservative gets even fair treatment. He gets trashed. I thank the *New York Times*' columnists and the mass media for proving my point that Walter Cronkite was a liberal from day one. I could not have done it without your help.

Now when Uncle Walter retired and tossed his purple mantle to Dan Rather (no one could ever call him Uncle Dan), only two things changed. What did not change was the liberal bias. But Dan was no Uncle Walter.

He was too arrogant or too dumb to wrap his bias with a little skill. The last thing one would pin on Rather was the word subtle.

In the bean-counting world, sometimes a business will engage in what's called "cooking the books." In the news business, Rather engaged in what I would call "cooking the news." Both are crimes in my opinion, with cooking the news far more dangerous. It leads to providing misinformation to the public, which leads to bad decisions by the public. Actually, cooking the news is propaganda, and one can easily see the results of propaganda in the November 2008 election results. Hitler and Goebbels were masters at news propaganda. Of course, they mastered the art with only simple tools, such as the radio, print media, and public demonstrations. No television was available to them. They were so effective with news management that even when Germany's cities were bombed to ruins and Allied troops were at the German borders, Hitler and Goebbels still controlled the minds of the masses. It could be happening here.

I ceased subscribing to *Time* and *Newsweek* long, long ago.

We no longer have a locally-owned and locally-operated newspaper. Both papers available on a daily delivery basis are published out of town and shipped in. Both papers are owned by large northern companies. It goes without saying that both are democrat (liberal) papers. Without exception the female columnists are liberal. Except for a few bones thrown to the conservatives in the form of a Cal Thomas, the male columnists are also democrats. Recently there was an article by a female columnist on the subject of the war on terror detainees. She flatly stated that their detention was wrong. No, she did not say that in her opinion it was wrong. She made the statement as if it were fact. It doesn't matter to her that I think she is dead wrong, but I don't have the power to reach so many people. So who gave her the authorization to make such an irresponsible public statement? The answer is the people that gave her a pen and a piece of paper, and then gave her the space to print such an opinionated and biased article. It is my considered opinion that this was not really her fault. After all, she is just doing what many girls do, throwing an emotional tantrum. The responsibility clearly lies with the owners of the paper. They knew exactly what they would get when they bought her, and they got it. Therefore, the paper has failed completely in its duty to fully inform the public on such important matters. Instead, it has presented its political agenda for its own self-centered purposes. Is it any wonder the newspapers are slowly committing suicide? The way they are today, I'm willing to do my part to help them—although it is possible BHO will bail them out, being a friend of the family and all that stuff, you know.

One does not have to be free of bigotry, hate, or lying to get a pass from the media for a gaffe at a public speech or private conversation. All one has to do is be politically correct, i.e., a radical or liberal. Within a few weeks of his inauguration in January 2009, the new president gave the media several opportunities to treat him as they did the non-politically correct. The media even helps him with his explanation if he doesn't get it quite right. They will add "no harm done," or "he did not mean it that way," or "he was just joking," et cetera, et cetera. Best of all, however, is hit it once and then drop it. It becomes an instant non-issue. Not so with the politically straight people. For an equally innocent comment, Trent Lott got hounded out of office. He is not alone. Just recently a female who was being interviewed on one of the networks spewed forth her hate, anger, and venom when she referred to people at an Atlanta Tea Party gathering as racist and rednecks. Except for Fox news, she got a pass from the media, and the reason is that "redneck" is not a politically incorrect term. In the media tradition, it refers to the straight white male from the South. And I might add, because they would, who drives a pickup. Now had she said "nigger," the world would have been up in arms.

ASSASSINATION BY MEDIA

To note a few: Richard Nixon. Poor ole Nixon

Lyndon Johnson, even though he did more for civil rights than any other president, the media detested him for taking Camelot's job and because they considered him a southern hick.

Dan Quayle. I met Quayle years ago, before he was trashed by the media. He appeared to me to be a solid citizen. Could that be the reason the media trash people such as Quayle, President Bush, and Sarah Palin? In fact, that is all the media looks for to trash a personality. The larger the threat to the liberal agenda, the more vitriolic the attack. The mass media views Palin as a major threat, and thus their irrational attacks. Please note that they never unleashed their heavy venom on McCain. That is because they never perceived him as a significant threat, and the reason they steered the GOP into nominating him.

George Bush, the younger

Sarah Palin, Big threats generate automatic, big defensive mechanisms

Assassination by the media is a political assassination normally. However, for Bush, the younger, and Palin, the media hatred (or fear) is so vicious that for some left wingers, simple political assassination may not satisfy their thirst.

Then there are those that get a free pass from the media. Some of these are:

John Kennedy—the eastern dandy and old money

Ted Kennedy—just the last name

Jimmy Carter. As the "new South" and with his ally, the news media, they poisoned the public on nuclear power. This wimp pussyfooted around with Iran for 444 days for zip, while Reagan took an hour and a half to cure this Carter abscess.

Bill Clinton—the new South II. Had this guy not been one of the protected species (i.e., a democrat), he would have been tossed out of office by the media quicker than they tossed out poor ole RN. Actually, he never would have been elected.

Al Gore—dumb

Joe Biden—dumber

Janet Reno—Texas massacre hero

John and Teresa Kerry—they deserve each other

Footnote: The above list begs for the two most recent protected guys, BHO and MO. When MO came across the screen as seething with hate and resentment, the media immediately curtailed her visibility. Democrat motto: Never run for office with your own clothes on. Don the moderate cloak if you want to get elected. Bill and Hill, Reno, Ginsberg, BHO,

MO—anything but moderates. To a man, all are 1960s-era left-wing radicals.

That the media detested Nixon is no question. However, not with the degree of hatred (or fear) invoked by Bush, the younger, or Palin. In Nixon's case, words such as *hateful* and *visceral* come to mind. But with Bush and Palin, words like *catatonic* and *vindictive* surface. Have the media turned even further to the left, or have they become bolder, more confident that no matter what they say or do, no one is going to reel them in and hold them accountable? The courts have permitted them to go overboard far beyond reason or justice. Once again, the "fair" test fails. The courts are largely responsible. Yes, the Constitution stipulates freedom of speech, and that is fine. However, the courts have also made it very difficult, if not impossible, for an off ended party to get redress. If there is going to be unbridled free speech, fine, but let the speaker be held accountable if he damages others. The courts, in fact, have done this in a few cases. E.g., threats or dangerous comments regarding air travel, and threats against some public officials. The courts need to revamp their hard line in other areas to yield a more responsible and, yes, a better, more accurate, and more responsible media. After all, their whole reason for being should be justice.

DOUBLE STANDARD

Only the astute observer will be alarmed by the double standards practiced by democrats. Mostly this is due to the fact that the media make nothing of democrat misconduct. Therefore, the masses are not made aware that democrats are guilty of conduct that, if done or said by a non-democrat, would be spread and condemned all over the media and repeated ad nauseam.

President Bush was unmercifully attacked verbally and in writing, in the most vicious language. He was and is even now called a liar. It was clear that the media hated Bush and his administration, and throughout his entire second term trashed him and his administration. The media aggravated the misconduct by not condemning it. A close observer will see that on any issue, the democrat will hold himself to a loose, mild, or no standard of conduct, while screaming bloody murder over a non democrat's minor infraction of the same thing.

And still the democrats make a big deal over two little words directed at BHO: "You lie." A famous ruler once said, "Word breaking [lying] is hideous in a ruler." That famous ruler was Genghis Kha Khan. I say Representative Wilson acted out of righteous indignation, and further, I believe him.

I place no credibility in anything that comes out of BHO's mouth. He has, by act or speech, told so many half-truths. His arrogance is such that he believes the masses will buy anything he says, even if it's180 degrees off what he said an hour earlier.

If BHO is not a foreigner, how could he get a scholarship reserved for foreigners? (Because he was black, of course, and was propelled along for affirmative action reasons.) If he is a foreigner, how could he be born in this country? Was he living a lie then or is he living a lie now? It has to be one or the other. And the mass media, except for one outlet, turned their backs to this story.

BHO is simplistic to the extreme. In a speech he can state anything that is already known to the entire world with such conviction, that it appears that this jewel has just been revealed to him for the first time, and now he is eager to share his newfound wisdom with the rest of the world. Duh?

As this document was being finalized for publication, publishers wanted to make sure it contained no "hate speech." I could not find that term in any available dictionary. It again appears to be an invention of the media, the minorities, and the courts. Even today there was a big to-do on the television about some guy that had made some remarks about not liking a female worker's attire, or something of that nature. The discussion on the television was about whether or not the guy was guilty of sexual harassment, hate speech, or even of violating the law. Of course he was guilty of none of those things. The guilty parties were the discussers, for they were attempting to deny this guy his freedom of speech.

Let's step aside here for an observation. On national television, two gals and a guy are attempting to categorize some guy's comments about a girl's attire. I am pretty good in math, and I put two and one together and came up with zero. Here's how. I couldn't care less what the guy said about the girl's dress, even if he said she looked like a hoer, or he repeated it a thousand times, or he said she would have looked better naked. Conversely, I couldn't care less if the girl made equally sharp comments about the guy. This guy and gal may have a spot on national television, but they are nothings. Nothings. That tells us something about the net worth of most television (not in terms of dollars), for the two girls and a guy are using the national airways to discuss trivia. Or if there is anything less than trivia, perhaps it is minutiae. The yap-yap of the two females is understandable; but how did they rope this adult male into joining them?

The country is lost in the jungle of democrat infantile fantasy with two-hundred-foot precipices all around, and I am not sure there are twelve clearheaded men in the entire District of Columbia who have the backbone to lead us back to base camp safely. Yet there they are on nationwide television, taking up time discussing some guy's comments about some gal's dress. As stated, two plus one equals zero. It could be less than zero, for it wastes the time of people with an IQ over one hundred. For those under one hundred, it is probably on a par with the typical sitcom, Oprah, and the stand-up comedians.

Building on that, the guy who is under fire from the PC Gestapo probably said no more than 100,000 guys say every day, myself included. I routinely comment to my lovely wife on the offensive attire of some females. She almost always agrees. And yes, it could be that some guy's attire is the target of the same sharply honed insight. If it is offensive to the eye and the mind, male or female, the observing eye is fair and balanced. It happens more frequently with females and is more offensive, because they get their marching orders from some wacky fashion fad, which they appear compelled to follow. Meanwhile, some guys get their direction from a movie, a comic strip, or a noir shop specializing in punk. It's called free speech! Is someone going to send out the politically correct Gestapo? If there is a law somewhere that states that such chatter is illegal, that law is unconstitutional. It's called free speech. Television has a big mouth, but some of us are going to continue to call a pig a pig, and if it is a fat dirty pig, we may even say that also. How about them apples? Sadly it is understood that the company fired the guy for his remarks about the girls attire. In effect they denied him his right of free speech. He should sue the company for damages.

And what gives me the ability to judge something unconstitutional? Believe it or not, this old southern boy can read, write, and do arithmetic. Plus, he has a clearer eye on what constitutes fair and justice, more than the Supreme Court does in many cases.

From my observation, whatever the definition of free speech, it is fluid. It depends not only on what was said, but who or what it was said about and who said it—at least three variables. Now the legislators have come up with a law that doubles the penalty for "hate acts," whatever they are, and some judge is going to decide whether or not one is guilty of a "hate crime" and lock one up for it double-time. Talk about unconstitutional. That is eyeball to eyeball with it. It is equal protection down the tubes.

Some years ago a controversy developed over some guy who had, under the sacred name of art, displayed a figurine of Christ in a container of urine. As I recall, this outrageous and hateful act was displayed in some art show in New York (but it could have been Washington, Chicago, or San Francisco), a show that might have been sponsored by the NEA. At some point this monstrosity was allowed to stand, because some judge decided that it fell under the freedom of expression or freedom of speech protection. Now, had the jar of urine contained a figurine of Mohammed, Martin Luther King, Jr., or BHO, that would probably come under the category of a "hate act" and would never have been permitted. But wait, did we not just say that it was allowed by a judge under the protection of free speech? But Christ in a bottle of urine is okay, because Christians are not one of the "protected" species. Protected meaning, protected by the courts, the media, and the minorities. Case closed.

BACKLASH: A POWERFUL WEAPON

Once again, with Sonia Sotomayer the media panned the right with an all-out assault on their attack of her record. "Better be careful, you'll be sorry," is their theme song when one of their protected ones come under fire. But for President Bush, Governor Palin, and others of the right, there is no such problem. The dolts Gore and Biden and others never got their just deserts. Clinton never got his, the guy the media put in the White House in November of 2008 never got his. This is because the network news anchors, the columnists, the talk show hosts, the editorialists have said, "Better watch out." Sotomayer publically proclaimed her superiority over the white male, and got a pass by a media that would have had apoplexy if the reverse had been pronounced.

Actually, this woman should never have been nominated for the Supreme Court, let alone confirmed. And it really has nothing to do with a white male. She disqualified herself when she basically said she would rule on her background and experience, rather than the Constitution.

Bush, Palin, and others of the right have been and still are assaulted without restraint, because they are not one of the media's protected persons. In fact, to the mass media they are equivalent to, if not in fact, the enemy, and therefore anything goes.

When one of the protected persons puts his foot in his mouth, which they always do when they are not reading the cue cards, the media will help by providing excuses, which range from "Oh, it was taken out of context," to "He didn't mean it that way," and "It was an honest mistake and could happen to anyone," et cetera.

We know there is a controlled and managed society in progress today. It is only acceptable to be politically correct. Any other position is wrong, according to the democrats.

With a half dozen or so of BHO's appointees having a history of failure to pay their income taxes, the administration and the loving media fell all over themselves to excuse and minimize the failure. The opponents blinked.

The backlash is only one of the many ways the media controls and manages society, and it is a powerful weapon. For the media can manufacture a backlash where one does not exist, if it so desires. And to silence an opponent, all it has to do is raise the bugaboo of a backlash. Knowing well the political position and power of the media, the opponent will usually soften his approach or withdraw altogether. If that fails, the media can always use the weapon of political correctness.

In one of the papers distributed locally by the newspaper syndicate, a large, liberal southern newspaper, the black female columnist referred to a former Republican congressman (white male) as a "fringe lunatic." Do you believe she had a fear of a backlash or of court action? I don't think so.

REVERSE LYNCHINGS

There are countless examples of some people charging whites (men) with offenses against blacks without the slightest bit of information. There is JJ, AS, and the latest, BHO. When a black screams that a white has committed an offense against them, these people go into an automatic diatribe against the accused. Even when they have been proven wrong time and again, and the white(s) is found innocent, it never even slows them down. They stay the course. (Could this be a revenue generating tactic?) The latest with JJ is his comparison of convicted animal cruelty guy, MV, with Jackie Robinson. There has to be very low IQ or a dollar reason. Of course, there is also the guy the media put in the White House in November 2008. Without any more information than JJ or AS, but with the identical mentality, BHO jumps in with both feet and charges a white policeman with acting stupidly. Now, he did have the policeman over for tea and crumpets, but he never apologized. And he did not apologize for the same reason that JJ and AS never apologized. First, they are not going to apologize to a straight white male. Second, they are not going to give any impression that they are and have been wrong, and are guilty of the worst kind of racism. Not that it needs highlighting. But when a brother Muslim killed thirteen and wounded thirty, BHO says, "Let's not rush to judgment." But with a white cop and black friend, the white cop is 75 percent wrong coming out the gate. Whatever happened to that twelve-person panel they appointed to "investigate" the arrest?

By now one would have thought that the first two members of this unholy trio would have learned to keep their big mouths zipped until they had some facts, but no. They convict the accused without benefit of jury, judge, or defense. Something other than reason or intelligence must drive that, like perhaps money On the other hand, I could be wrong. It could be a lack of one or all three of the above. One cannot expect too much of the third member of this unholy alliance, as he was put in office by a loving media and cue cards. One news outlet reported BHO has been noting the misspeaks by his own selected VP. There were public notations long before his selection that Joe wasn't all there. So BHO, please don't be too harsh on your personally appointed man, as he has not had the benefit of 100 percent cue-card performances; and it has been shown that when you don't have a cue card, you perform no better. Get it, "stupidly"? Although you hide it quite well, I believe your loyalty to the United Sates is no different than that of JJ, AS, or MO. It may be observed that while BHO will at least acknowledge the verbal errors of his white male VP, he will acknowledge no such offense with his black brothers or for himself.

On his first trip abroad after being installed in the White House by the media, the media's boy refused to bow to England's Queen, yet did bow to the king of an Islamic country. Later he bowed deeply to the Japanese emperor. At this point, I am uncertain whether that is the ultimate political correctness or the ultimate in stupidity. On second thought; however, it is probably the ultimate in both. And the bow is on video. The White House spokesman denied he bowed, yet there it was for the world to see. Could he have dropped a penny on the floor and only stooped to pick it up? One must carefully consider the many possibilities of the definition of "is" when dealing with a democrat. But with the bow to the Japanese emperor, clearly there was no penny on the floor.

Within weeks of the democrats seizing control of two branches of the federal government in 2009 (they already own 4/9 of the Supreme Court), the newly appointed Homeland Security Secretary, Janet Napolitano, issued the agency's intelligence assessment, in which returning veterans were classified as right-wing extremists or potential terrorists. And to a committed left-wing radical, that is exactly what they are. Now, make no mistake about it. The words were not put down in error, nor were they an oversight or unintentional. That's the way a left-wing democrat (I repeat myself) really feels. Never thought they would put it in writing for the world to see, however. How dare they use their hatred of the military to demonize America's citizen soldiers? This is mass indictment, targeting and profiling, and all those other evils they so recently hung the Bush administration out to dry for. The people responsible for such outrage are unbalanced. As a thinking person would expect, the worst terrorist attack on our soil came not from a returning veteran, but an Islamic extremist in military uniform who had never served overseas. Believe it.

REVERSE/ PERMISSIBLE DISCRIMINATION

In 2009 Rush Limbaugh was asked to be a partner in the purchase of a professional football franchise. Some may remember that when it was made public, a minority-generated firestorm erupted. In the resulting politically correct nightmare, Rush was asked to withdraw from the partnership due to the tantrums of AS, JJ, the football players association (large number of minorities there), and NFL officials. Now what was this all about? Bottom line: Rush is a conservative radio talk show host, and that makes him politically incorrect. Therefore for Rush, the price of political incorrectness is denial of an opportunity to participate in a business venture.

Although some left-wing nuts throw out some crazy quotes that they attributed to Rush, no one could show them to be true. In fact, the research showed them to be untrue. As I see it, it was an open and shut case of reverse and permissible discrimination—but that's okay for a white guy. Rush did make a negative comment about the ability of a black football player years before, and he might have survived that. His fatal mistake, however, was that he tied the player's questionable ability with a media bias toward said player. Thus, in one stroke he alienated the black players and the media, a powerful combination. And they "done him in." Another prime example of the power of political correctness to control free speech. Except for one TV channel, there was no cry of outrage from anyone else. Most appeared to feel Rush simply got his just due for being politically incorrect. It's all about intimidating people by political correctness, a shame upon our nation. Free speech denied.

CHANGE

For a democrat to have a burning desire to change something, such as health care, it is not necessary for him to know how to correct it. His attitude is, "I don't care what it is or what it costs or the total impact on the citizens as a whole. Just change it." That it might be ten times worse doesn't bother him in the least. Of course, the current administration is not the first to be unhappy with the health care system (or is it power, or is it race?). When Bill and Hill got in office, I'm not sure about Bill, but Hill was so unhappy with the health care status quo, she crashed and burned, and they had to exile her, much as they did with MO after her "first time proud" speech.

That this is a pure power play is unquestioned. Rather than provide coverage for the uncovered, which is the easiest possible solution to this democrat bellyache, the democrats want to revamp the system for all 350 million of us. Once again, doesn't take a genius to see that this is not about health care coverage.

All 350 million—except, that is, members of Congress and many federal executives. These privileged people are not about to put themselves on the same health care plan as the masses. The masses. Well, that's you and I.

JUST ANOTHER WELFARE PROGRAM:

The democrats are beating the drum even still on "health care reform." But it is not really health care reform, for reform means to change and improve. Whatever they do to the staggering cost of health care, they are not really going to do anything significant about health care cost. They are not going to do anything significant about tort reform and the huge lawyer fees. No, these guys pay off the democrats with campaign contributions, their support, and their votes. Cost-cutting will never happen. The democrats are not going to do anything significant about enormous doctor fees, which are in large part attributable to the lawyer. Never happen. The democrats are not going to do anything significant about the outrageous hospital costs. These costs are driven by highly-paid hospital administrators and highly-paid staff. Add to that overly generous pension plans and benefit packages, which are driven in large part by unions. Hospital administrators know that whatever cost increases they yield to the unions won't come out of their pockets. These costs will just be passed on to the taxpayer or insured patient. (This is another reason public employees should not be allowed to unionize.) The democrats are not going to change anything significant with the insurance companies, because in large part their costs are driven by the lawyer cost, the doctor cost, and the hospital cost, and we have already seen that that just "ain't gonna" happen.

So what is the democrats' "health care reform" all about? It is just another welfare program and vote-buying scheme. Although the media and democrats insist that health care is a right, it is not. Nor is the welfare state in any form a right. In fact, it is wrong, unless a compassionate people that can afford it from the fruits of their labor can see a valid need, and address that need on a volunteer basis.

BUT NOTHING EVER CHANGES THE LIBERALS

Over one hundred years ago, a famous British soldier, statesman, and author observed, following a successful military campaign, that the Liberals suggested they "would have shown such tact in their diplomacy that war might possibly have been avoided altogether and all its objects ... would have been achieved without shedding blood." Well, it didn't work for Neville Chamberlain, it didn't work for Jimmy Carter (444-day Carter), it didn't work for Bill and Hill, and it hasn't worked for BHO. Now there is an area begging for change—their own mentality.

MORE ON CHANGE

For someone who grew up in the '40s and '50s, most of the things of today would have been thought impossible at that time. That is, had they been thought of at all. The fact is, they were so far the other side of impossible, they were not thought of. I am not referencing technological changes here. The democrat cry for change is endless, if one thinks about it, for it is a self-interest change, a fantasy-world change he is looking for--actually, an egalitarian society where equal participation, reason, love, cooperation, and peace prevail. No voice need be raised, no quarrel need exist, no water disturbed, for all would be in harmony; and every need, if not desire, would be promptly satisfied.

Well, world, wake up! Science and technology have made magnificent advances in the last century, but human nature ... Well, human nature is still a hundred years later basically unchanged. If anything, it may have regressed, and if that's true, we can thank the democrats, the television, and the courts for that.

These days the "unthinkable," the "never happen" and "impossible" and "you 're crazy" of yesterday is an everyday event. See, not all change is for the good.

DEFENDING THE INDEFENSIBLE

Let's presume there may be situations or areas of public affairs where democrats have at least a plausible argument. On the other hand, there are more situations or areas of public affairs where they should be speechless or yield to common sense, but they don't. Because if they did, their entire house of cards would come tumbling down. So they vehemently defend the indefensible. Even where the situation is so obviously true that if it would not destroy their fantasy world, reason would dictate that they agree, and they would agree—but not at the expense of political correctness. They are willing to look ridiculous to maintain their politically-correct agenda. Except for Fox, television news permits the liberals to get by with such crazy positions, either by not putting the questions to their fellow travelers, or by not pointing out the holes in their defense. In a way, their defense is like a dam. If a tiny hole develops in the heart of a dam, it is just a matter of time before the whole structure collapses. So they deny the hole. In fact, if necessary to defend their position, they will deny the dam.

But one can *never* persuade anyone to give up their "freebies" (that is, entitlements) by reason or logic.

In June 2009 a guest columnist wrote a newspaper article on the subject of the white man becoming a minority by the year 2042. The article was on the editorial page and was written by a white male who, as I recall, had at one time served as mayor of a New England city. What struck me was that I got the impression this dolt was delighted with the possibility, or even probability, of that coming to pass.

This whiz kid is behind his IQ power curve, since in practice if not in numbers, the white male is already a minority in this politically correct society. There is even a female of Hispanic ancestry on the U.S. Supreme Court who testified to that. Further, the rebuttal to her statements have been minimal for two reasons. One, the mass media is in bed with her; and two, the opposition is cowed by mortal fear of a backlash. No guts, no glory.

Let's have a round of applause for the white male. Contrary to today's misrepresentation, the white male is not all bad. Believe it. A bow to all participants, from pioneer, farmer, soldier, inventor, rancher, craftsman, educator, scientist, industrialist, entertainer, doctor, nurse, mother, minister and steel worker. All made a contribution to bring this country to its glory years. But it was the white male that led the charge in this country's founding, its wars, its inventions, its government, its education, its industry, its power. He led it all and he did a great job. His biggest failure is that in his grace and good will, he allowed internal rot to get a foothold and then explode in his face. Now, is that a nice piece of political incorrectness or not? Two can play the political propaganda game.

It is only in a politically correct nation, such as the late great United States of America, that the whining of the minorities has been allowed to control all branches of the federal government. Again, this could not be done without the help of the courts and the media.

Who can figure a democrat? Their refusal to answer a direct question with a direct response is a continuing joke. Instead of a *yes* or *no*, they just give a little speech that doesn't say anything, or they are bouncing off the wall. This phenomenon can be attributed to several possible personal problems by the democrat.

1. Ignorance of the entire picture, with all the accompanying consequences of individual actions
2. Inability to deal with the "other side of the coin"
3. Possibly vaguely aware that acknowledging another side would make them look stupid or foolish
4. They are self-centered beyond belief.
5. Inability to change their position, therefore feeling that would mean they had/were wrong in their former position. All their other positions would be in question.
6. They live in a world of make-believe, a fantasy island, an infantile playpen.
7. Their minds are closed to any other option than their own position.
8. Their method of operation has emotion as its source.

When a democrat is lacking any rational argument against an issue, he almost invariably attacks the spokesman. They seek to belittle, discredit, or ridicule the brave worrier, knowing that on the issue, they can never win the battle of common sense in the heart of the informed citizen. For this reason, their cohorts in the media pick up on the personal attack and never point out that the issue itself has been totally dropped from visibility

In reality, there is nothing wrong with a democrat answering a direct question with a direct response, and then giving his own rationale for whatever position he espouses. Is that because if he answers the question straightforwardly, he might waver in his position?

It is apparent to anyone with an ounce of common sense that so-called same-sex marriages or relationships of any manner go against nature. The master design gives a male definite mental and physical attributes, as it does the female. These are different attributes, however. The male does not possess the female accommodations, and the female does not possess the male accommodations. This design, by the way, is perfect to accomplish its intended purpose. Anything different goes against the master design and nature. For those who might not quite get it, here is a word picture. Take two bolts and two nuts. In mechanics, one is commonly called a male piece and the other a female piece (common terminology in electrical, plumbing, et cetera). Examine each piece and you should get the picture why each is called what it is. The bolt is male, the nut female. Now it is obvious two bolts cannot mate (or marry), nor can two nuts mate (or marry). There may be some weird things they can do together, but they cannot mate. Some may call it an "alternate" lifestyle, but not so. It is a deviation of nature.

A DEMOCRAT ALSO:

Is a person that would never see the gap in effect between the big stick and the big talk. During the reign of a democrat president, Iran took a large number of Americans hostage. This democrat president was all talk. At the end of 444 days, apparently he still had not come up with the right words to the Iranians, as they still refused to release the hostages. It is no coincidence that within hours of Reagan assuming the presidency, the American hostages held by the terrorist state were all released. Now I do not know what Reagan said to the Iranians, but one can bet his life savings it wasn't, "Let's get together, hold hands, sing songs, and dance around the maypole." It was probably "Look, buster, release in twenty-four hours or your ass is grass." Big stick.

It is no accident that the bombing under another democrat president of a U.S. warship that went unpunished only resulted in more bombing. It is no accident that not long after the assumption of the presidency by a Republican, Muslim terrorists struck the worst blow by an outside enemy in the history of our country (9/11), but this time the terrorists got a different response. They had handed to them retribution, swift retribution. Since that time there has not been a single attack on our shores, until another democrat (BHO) was put in the White House by the media. Not only that, but some of the safeguards against our enemies dismantled under democrat presidents have been activated again. A big stick at work. Terrorists understand force. Again, it is no accident that within days of another democrat assuming the presidency and halting the trial of a terrorist, another terrorist in another country with which this country has conflict was released from arrest—and the country was only in the early days of this democrat presidency. Even as this is written, administration forces and their supporters are active in betraying our core intelligence organization. It appears that this green president does not have the intelligence to see that terrorists love to deal with "softies." They are free to play their game without worry of retaliation. Terrorist states over the globe favored the democrat over the Republican in the last presidential election. They would love nothing more than to see captured terrorists thrown into the morass of our legal system. (Notice I did not say justice system. The justice element went away long ago.) True stories all.

There is ample evidence that some minorities in this country sympathize with the terrorist Islamic element. In the November 2008 election, for example, the democrat element spoke against Israel and expressed sympathy for the Muslims (indicating the problem may be *us*), and yet most Jews voted for the democrat candidate. Although people classified as Jews have traditionally supported minority causes, minorities as a class are anti-Israel and anti-war if it is directed to the Islamic elements. They were pro-war, however, in the Bosnia/Serbia conflict.

Some evidence is also found in their adoption of Arabic names and the Muslim religion. More is provided by their sympathies with Muslim causes. More is provided by appointees in the BHO administration. Why would these minority officials specify that Islamic terrorists should be tried in the civil court mess, unless they were sympathetic to the Islamic cause and wanted to help them escape justice? Traditionally, these people are tried in a military court. There could be another motive, and that is that they see this as a white man's cause. Therefore, any foe of the white man is a friend of the minority. There is even another possibility, and that is that the minorities are almost universally against punishment of a minority for any and all crimes, including murder. Another possibility, and possibly the correct one, is that they don't have a clue about what they are doing. Or could it be an on-the-job training program for trial lawyers at the public's expense? I can easily believe any and all of the above.

A democrat is also a person who has for years rejoiced with the liberal/radical elements, making the WASP the butt of jokes, sarcasm, and anything and everything that they saw as obstructing their dreams of Utopia. Today, that acronym is outdated, for it has been expanded to include Catholics and narrowed to exclude the homosexual. That would make today's politically correct term WECS, i.e., White, European, Christian, Straight; and, truth winning out, mostly Male, for many WECS females vote with the liberals (as can be seen from the last presidential election). That would make the term WECSMM, the MM being Mostly Male. The liberals/radicals have untold hatred for this group, for it is the only barrier to their fantasy world of no rules, no responsibility, no borders, and no brains. Should anyone doubt the validity of this scenario, one only has to watch the network evening news for just one day. Get the picture. This specific group, the WECSMM, almost universally oppose the liberal elements in their hatred of the military, war, nuclear power, abortion rights, gun control, freedom, the U.S., et cetera.

Is a person that surely would never have listened to the late Paul Harvey. The last thing they want to hear is "the rest of the story," and they find it impossible to speak it themselves. They thrive on that part of the story that fits their purpose and the devil take the rest of the story. They repeat it endlessly, and perhaps throw in an example from fifty, one hundred, or two hundred years ago that may or may not be applicable to the discussion. It is strictly a surface game, totally lacking in depth. It is unclear when and where this uniquely democrat/liberal mentality (or lack thereof) came from, but probably the most visible and famous example of that trait is the Lincoln Memorial. In it one will find carved in stone some very high-sounding (and highly selected) words. But if one were to read the entire text (i.e., the rest of the story), he would walk away with an entirely different conclusion. Could this selected piece of the puzzle account for why the democrat is unable to face the truth, the whole truth, and nothing but the truth, and therefore is totally unequipped to see the total picture (which one could call reality)?

Is a person that will vigorously support the most vile, repulsive, disrespectful, and unnatural of words and deeds with one hand, while with the other hand condemning Christianity and anything decent.

Is a person that can condemn and picket a cigarette smoker; yet advocate legalizing marijuana. Go figure.

Is a person that can advocate abortion of a human child; yet condemn a person that squashes a darter snail or advocates capital punishment. Again, with a straight face.

Is a person of so narrow a view of life that he cannot clearly see the road ahead, let alone the big picture. You can call that tunnel vision.

Is a person so transfixed by his own self-centeredness that he cannot acknowledge even a thought that he might be wrong. Usually, of course, he is.

Is a person that gives no thought to how dishonest it is to pass himself off as a sheep if it will win him an election. That is fraud.

Is a person that will vote for any measure, no matter how harmful to the majority, if he feels it will benefit him or gain him votes. No joke here!

Is a person that doesn't care if you murdered your grandmother and buried her in the backyard, so long as you vote for democrats and democrat programs. Please, let's get our priorities straight.

Is a person that can call years of failure to pay income taxes an "honest mistake" with a perfectly straight face. And if he is a cabinet nominee, convince the IRS not to charge interest nor invoke a penalty. (The rest of us would be in deep stuff, and still he gets the cabinet appointment).

Is person that, reading this little book, will describe it as insensitive, lacking in diversity, not inclusive, anti-abortion, uncaring, reactionary, and environmentally unfriendly.

Is a person that should be required to read the fine print of the French Revolution down to the very last murder. If that fails, he should try the fine print of the rise and decline of the Roman Empire. If *that* fails, there is no hope of his ever being a balanced person. Assuming, of course, he can read.

Is a person that views the world and all the institutions and agencies therein from a victim mentality. That is, unless it is a doer of a crime. In that case, the doer of the crime becomes the victim, and the real victim of the crime is of no consequence, even after rape, assault, robbery, and murder. Obviously it is his or her fault for being at the wrong place at the wrong time.

Is a person that will advocate the banning of guns for the law-abiding majority, while offering nothing to keep them out of the hands of the criminal element. They are unable to see that terrorists and criminals can get guns if they want at any time.

Is a person that has forgotten (or never learned) that history is self-

correcting, in its own time and way. And that it is cyclical for an indefinite period. Something about reaping what you sow.

Is a person who participates in or conducts closed meetings at which they condemn others for being exclusionists. Some state legislatures have a black caucus. Should someone start up a white caucus, they would scream "racist," and the media and the courts would back them up.

Is a person that can ask a twelve-year-old daughter what she thinks of nuclear war. (Stay at least one hundred miles away from a person dumb enough to ask that question of anyone, let alone a twelve-year old.) And that person was so proud of himself, he announced it on national television. True story.

Is a person that is unable to distinguish the difference between a nuclear bomb and an electric power station powered by nuclear energy. "A person" here could also mean the media.

Is a person incapable of answering a direct, sensible question—usually because he knows a direct, sensible answer will make him look like a fool. Another true story.

Is a person always ready to advocate change, so long as you don't ask him the details on how to do it and the ramifications of that change. They do it all the time.

Is a person that doesn't recognize his own contribution to damaging the environment. It's always someone else's doing. Ah, fantasy world.

Is a person that fails to see that whatever options exist with saving some part of the environment today, each and every one of them will be steamrolled over so long as the world population continues to grow. Prove me wrong.

Is a person that tosses rocks in the road to better law enforcement and whines about the ratios of minorities in the prison compared with the population—while still crying about all the crime on the streets. The thought apparently never comes to these people that minorities are in prison in that ratio because they commit the crimes in that ratio. Even in today's paper, a writer was whining about the ratio of minority congressional

members under investigation. I suppose the cure for that is to investigate a sufficient number of non-minority members just to get a pleasing ratio. To repeat myself: low IQ.

Is a person that advocates charity by the government and individuals, but declines to contribute his portion.

Is a person that drives to the grocery store in a Cadillac to get his groceries with food stamps, and yet sees no contradiction in that. Doesn't everybody have a Cadillac?

Is a person that no matter what is given to him, wants more and more and more. No place for jokes here.

Is a person that can figure out how to finagle $250,000 Katrina grant money out of the government, yet can't figure out how to get a job. Not just one incident either. In the newspaper delivered here, there was recently an article that a couple of minority females that were employed by a government emergency management agency were indicted for embezzling over $700,000 from the agency. The two apparently diverted agency funds to accounts held in the names of relatives and friends. In large part, these sort of frauds, discovered by audit agencies, happen because of the government's near panic to get bucks into the pockets of minorities. Therefore, minorities are given passes in the form of not being held to the same standards as a straight white male, or perhaps not being held to any standard. In none of these cases since the Katrina storm have I read of a single dollar being recovered.

Is a person that can elect or reelect to public office a fellow democrat doing prison time for such crimes as drugs, embezzlement, or fraud. Of course, remember from Bill and Hill that character doesn't count.

Is a person better at working his tongue than his brain or body. Think about it.

Is a person with money enough to go to Washington, DC, on a "protest" march, yet can't seem to pay his bills without government support. Only makes sense to a democrat.

Is a person that can put a $6,000 paint job and $3,000 custom wheels and rims on a $3,000 car, with the title in hock to a loan shark, while getting his food with food stamps and living in government-subsidized housing. Of course, he can get the $3,000 wheels and rims on a monthly rental basis if he lacks ready cash or credit. Again, only makes sense to a democrat.

Is a person that refuses to come to terms with cold, brutal facts. It's just too painful and so much fun to be politically correct.

Is a person that can deny the obvious —and do it with a perfectly straight face. Would you agree the word *fake* is appropriate?

Is a person that believes government money can correct any and all social issues. The more money the better; there can't be enough. It is too painful to face the facts.

Is a person that lives in a fantasy world. Educated by the lowest form of programs on the television and what is left of the dying newspaper industry, they live in the company of soap operas, Oprah, so-called reality shows, and sitcoms that requiring only an IQ of eighty-five to comprehend. Actually, the media is largely responsible for creating this fantasy world.

Is a person that still believes there can be such a thing as an egalitarian society. Probably the two most familiar attempts at such a society are Russia and China. Both communist regimes started out as dictatorial police states, severely restricting personal freedom and personal initiative. Both are dismal failures. The third example, France, is probably not known to most democrats.

Is a person that will accuse others of violating the rights of man even while he is violating the rights of man.

Is a person with little or no knowledge or understanding of history, except isolated, self-interest elements.

Is a person that thinks of himself as super-normal rather than abnormal. He is good at self-deception, but poor at self-examination.

Is a person with an axe to grind, or perceived grievance to correct, a holy mission, a handicap of some sort, mental or physical, to make up for.

Is a person that will bomb or mob a school in protest of some perceived injustice, yet will mob the state legislature the next day to blackmail them into sending more money to the schools.

Is a person that cannot see that beyond a certain level, the money per student expenditure has nothing to do with the quality of education a student will receive.

Is a person that when asked a question he does not want to answer, will speak about the weather in Bermuda for ten minutes. By then, folks would not dare repeat the question.

Is a person that will elect or reelect to office an individual sitting in jail for some crime. Not a chance one would hear of a Republican doing that, for the media, while perhaps repeating the democrat situation, do not condemn it. But the Republican knows he would get executed by the media.

Is a person that sees no crime if the perpetrator is a fellow traveler.

Is a person either ignorant of history or refuses to accept it. He does not know that the "arsenal of democracy" did not necessitate appeasement. To the contrary, appeasement necessitated the arsenal of democracy. In every crisis there is always an element looking for "peace in our time"—at any price.

Is a person that does not know or will not face the fact that the only way to stop the human contribution to global warming is to stop humans from reproducing. All other activities so directed are merely window dressing.

Is a person that sees no parallel between Richard Nixon and Bill Clinton. Nixon was hounded out of office by the media. Clinton got a pass by the media because he was a fellow traveler. Had he been a Republican, he would have been run out of office too. In fact, with the Arkansas scandal exposed during his first run for the presidency, he would never have been

elected in the first place had the media not killed the story. Remember, in those days there was no Fox news.

Is a person that knows that television sells. No matter how it stinks, it can be sold if one is patient and keeps chipping away. How does a country go from men like Roosevelt, Truman, Eisenhower, Reagan, and George Bush to an Obama? This is how: the liberals put up a southerner, Carter, as a storefront, and he cracked the door by showing us that we just did not need much out of a president. Clinton flung the door wide open by showing us we did not need to expect anything from a president. So with the door wide open, it was easy for the media to install their boy in the White House. That's how one gets from Roosevelt/Eisenhower to an "obomanation."

Is a person that is totally unable to make the connection between the most heinous and brutal crime on an innocent victim and his family and the justice of capital punishment. I would call it the cause/effect principle, a very common scenario acted out in many areas of our society on a daily, if not hourly, basis. These same people, however, usually vehemently support abortion. Again, go figure.

Is a person that attempts to sell the public on the idea that progressive means whatever a liberal espouses. Actually, progressive means moving forward, as in advancing civilization. Most democrats' programs have nothing to do with advancing civilization.

Is a person that would rather send a welfare check to a person sitting in a subsidized house with subsidized air-conditioned comfort, munching on chips paid for by food stamps, watching some idiotic television program; rather than send a check for the same amount to a guy for work performed, such as building a road, a bridge, a ship, or some exportable product. Democrats are totally incapable of thinking in these terms. I am reminded of a young black guy that came to me years ago looking for a job. At the time, I had an opening for what I called a technician, someone to pass out and check in electronic instruments. The young man had a college degree from a black or predominately black college. I explained the job opening, and remarked that I did not know why the Employment Office had sent him to me. They knew I could not hire him, since his education made him overqualified, and that was the company policy as established by the Employment Office. At any rate, I sent him back to the Employment Office. The next day I got a call from that office. They indicated that the guy was threatening to make an issue out of the fact that I had an opening and would not hire him. I reminded them that that was their own policy (which they acknowledged). But, they added, he was threatening to make trouble, so couldn't I hire him? I stated I would and did. The young man did not stay long, but while he was there he did impart to some of the other technicians his feelings about his position in life. As reported to me, he told some of the other technicians that he shouldn't have to work for a living at all, and that white people should fully support him because "our fathers and grandfathers discriminated against his father and grandfather." Now, I do not believe this young man came up with this jewel himself. I strongly suspect he adopted this attitude about life because he had been taught it in scholastic and religious institutions he attended.

Is a person that would never see that on the scales of justice—not law, not precedence, not someone's idea of how society should be structured or should function, not an abortive attempt to compensate for some select acts of the past, not some totally unquantifiable environmental issue—but on the scales of justice, the democrat is consistently lacking; and that is because he, as a person, is lacking. A newspaper columnist recently opined that there was something ice-cold at the center of BHO. Possibly, it is more like a void. On a national scale the BHO administration is a perfect example of the net results of "affirmative action," "diversity," and "political correctness." It is the same mentality that has destroyed our public schools.

SOCIAL SECURITY: JUST ANOTHER WELFARE PROGRAM

Over the years, the democrats have repeatedly attempted to scare the daylights out of the voters with the tale that Republicans are going to cut Social Security, or that the Social Security bank was going broke under a Republican administration. To some degree, it had its intended negative impact on Republican candidates.

As in many other areas of our governmental affairs, the democrats are the guilty party for convoluting a respectable, even admirable, program. Social Security was originally passed as a small pension program for workers reaching retirement age, who otherwise would be without income in their old age. This program was partially financed by withholdings from workers' paychecks. There is nothing wrong with the Social Security bank, had the program been left as originally written. But along the way, the democrats have turned it into another welfare program. Today millions are drawing

Social Security, or getting other benefits from the program, that have never paid a single penny into the system. That is the reason the Social Security system is broke. Once again, the working class people are footing the bill for the welfare class.

At least for some, the government is not just spending tax revenue, it is actually using contributions paid in by workers for a welfare program without the approval of the workers. So if someday the retired worker has no old-age pension, it is because the government took his and others' contributions, and gave the money to people that never contributed anything to the system. Yet the working-class people have not rebelled. Is it because they have given up to an increasingly all-powerful federal overlord? And new health care reform? Well, it is not about health care. It is just another welfare program.

Actually, this is just a welfare program under cover of a worthwhile program—Social Security. If the government wanted to give these people money, it should have just created another welfare program for them. The government did not do that because, in part, it would make it easier for the public to see the various and gigantic welfare programs, and the total cost of these freeloaders. Another change to the Social Security system implemented by the government was, insult on insult, to implement an income tax on the old-age pension. It gives with one hand and takes away with the other.

In the late summer of 2009, BHO sent Social Security recipients notice that they would get no cost-of-living increase for two years. Has anyone heard even a whimper from the old folks? Hardly a month after this announcement, the president announced that he was cutting back on the federal employees' cost-of-living increase, from 2.4 percent to 2 percent, due to the economic situation. Frankly, I'm unimpressed. Why do the

federal workers making good salaries on the public payroll get a cost of living increase, when Social Security pensioners don't get a penny for two years? Oh, well, Congress is getting only 4 percent, so things are about right in a irresponsible way. Through all this, the people that have paid into the Social Security system have hardly lifted a finger or a curse.

The poor working stiff not only has to pay from his own pocket to help pay for his old-age pension, but then he has to pay income tax on his pension. By any name that's at least a double taxation. Why doesn't the government just reduce the Social Security checks by a percentage equal to their tax needs, and thus eliminate the Social Security income tax? But don't go there. There is a reason for that, and besides, the answer is un-American.

Democrats have a vast capacity for ignoring facts. They:

—can readily blank out 98 percent of the picture, only to focus on the 2 percent again and again.

—spread their propaganda readily, so that all have the same identical response to any attack. They can live or die standing on one pebble as their entire case.

—have condemned lynching over and over and over again, yet have no problem publicly lynching (using their friends, the media) without facts or without trial anyone they perceive as acting against them or a fellow traveler.

—have no problem using blackmail of businesses, organizations, or public officials to force their will upon them.

There are some things at which democrats are good. In fact, very good. One is the art of deception. Another thing is political correctness, which is a form of deception. A democrat will quickly lie to avoid being caught being politically incorrect. In a speech given in September 2009, the vice president, who was elected by the media in November 2008, made a reference to undocumented aliens. Of course, he was referring to illegal aliens in politically correct terminology. I suppose the reason for using the term "undocumented aliens" is that illegal aliens sounds so, well, so illegal. Besides, these are not pigs, they are votes. The definition of political correctness is any political position or term considered by a democrat to be acceptable (non-offensive to them or one of their various minority groups). Democrats consider all manner of things offensive, and for strange reasons.

In a recent sting operation involving ACORN employees, an ACORN employee advised a reporter posing as a prostitute to not use that term. She should use the term *performance artist* Instead. One must guard his speech for fear of off ending another or simply telling the truth. No more Polish jokes, no more ridiculing the ridiculous, no more sweet innocence, no more "meaning no offense" words.

One must never call a pig a pig, do not call a swine a swine, and for heaven's sake, don't use the term fat pig. Of course, it is okay to use the word in some contexts; e.g., capitalist pig, police pig, or Republican pig.

Just don't call a pig a pig.

UNCIVIL CONDUCT

Many years ago there was at a town meeting in south-central Pennsylvania, where the topic of discussion was nuclear power (as in electricity, not bombs).

The meeting was opened properly enough, and the anti-nuclear element (which was most of the room, and mostly female) spoke against nuclear power. Environmental organizations were participants. The speakers were passionate in presenting their views, but totally ignorant of facts. Theirs was a mindset of fear—fear of the unknown, such as has accompanied many technological breakthroughs, such as electricity.

When it finally came time for the pro-nuclear people to talk, the anti-nuclear mob came to life—catcalls, boos, shouting, and even some people mounting the speaker's platform to get within three or four inches of the speaker's face and shouting him down. In all my years, I had never witnessed such atrocious conduct by anyone. Needless to say, the meeting was finally aborted. This ugly scene did not make the national media,

because it would have made the anti-nukes look like fools, and the media was of the same mentality.

A few years later, there was another town meeting in south-central Mississippi, where a hearing was being held on the possible storage of nuclear waste in a salt dome. It turned out to be another chaotic, fear and ignorance driven event. During the meeting, a speaker from a national environmental group stated that the heat from the waste would be so great, it would "extend the growing season" at ground level. Now, this waste was going to be one half mile below the surface. Of course, the masses cannot be expected to know this is impossible, so it isn't their fault. It is the leaders and spokespeople of these irresponsible groups.

Another scene unfolded in south-central Mississippi, when an element at the University of Mississippi raised the red flag of deformed animals at a salt dome that had been used for an atomic test in the 1960s. Again, a national environmental group was involved in these allegations. Now in the blink of an eye, state and federal authorities were on the scene running tests, getting samples, and examining all sorts of wildlife, including turtle eggs. All results were negative. About the time the state governor arrived at the scene, information came in that there had apparently been an error in the data (due, as I recall, to a contaminated planchet) at the university. The governor got back in his big black car, and his highway patrol escorted him back to Jackson. The state and federal investigating teams folded their tents and went back to work. Again, this liberal fantasy never made the national media.

Given the mode of operation of liberals in disrupting meetings and events, and in deception, it is no wonder that Joe Wilson was driven to rise up and say, "You lie." How dare the liberals open their loud mouths? But, as stated, it is not necessary for liberals to be polite or politically correct. This form of misconduct by democrats is just another technique they employ to deny another's free speech, and is just as effective as intimidation by political correctness.

AMAZING GRACE

For generations now, the liberals have been known for their street-fighting techniques—marches, shouting, yelling down speakers, hissing, booing, personal assaults. You name it, they have engaged in it--even bombings, invasion of other people's property, disturbing the peace, intimidation, and blackmail. You name it, and they have engaged in it. The media, far from condemning these uncivil and criminal antics, have endorsed and encouraged them. Truth is, the media believes the targets of this hate, anger, and ridicule deserve every bit of it and more. Misinformation, malignancy, and maliciousness are all part of their plans.

Now comes Joe Wilson and his two little words, six letters in all. From out of the sewer crevices, from the four corners of the country, not to mention the democrat Congress and the liberal newspapers, comes a howl of "civility," to "settle our differences without shouting," to "be sweet, gentle, and loving." Such gall, but the democrats are too infantile to see the double standard. They invented the words *civil unrest*.

In their continuing condemnation of Joe Wilson, it appears every liberal columnist (and that is by far most of them) has to do an article condemning Joe. One columnist even went so far as to acknowledge the conduct of the left toward President Bush. His response to his own statement was: "Two wrongs don't make a right," thereby totally excusing the first wrong while damning the second! Why he would excuse the former and condemn the latter is not known. However, I suspect the thought process, conscious or subconscious, goes something like this. Now look here, you Republicans or Independents know better, therefore you are held to a higher standard. Those other folk cannot be expected to perform to your standard, because they are all handicapped in some way—economically, culturally, educationally, physically, or mentally—or they are undocumented (illegal) aliens. And thus to the liberal, anything and everything they do is okay, because they really don't know any better.

NOT ENVISIONED BY THE FOUNDING FATHERS

There is Diversity and then there is diversity.

The word from the democrats is that diversity is not just good, it's what makes us great. In line with the democrat agenda, diversity fits like a glove. But hold on. Diversity to the democrat means all types of races, all types of sexual preferences, all types of religions (or lack thereof), et cetera. But it does not include diversity of opinion or diversity of vote.

Briefly, the democrat does not care what kind of human makes the X on the ballot, so long as the X supports the party line. The democrats use diversity to push unqualified or less qualified people into jobs; to push less qualified or unqualified people into classrooms as students, as teachers, or as administrators; to punish corporations if they don't have at least one of every variety of human in their advertising, preferably with variety mixed/gender mixed hand holders. The democrats have sympathizers in the courts, in the media, and, of course, in their own ranks. What the democrats' version of diversity has wrought is a hardened line in the sand. At least in part, the citizens outside the democrat camp see that the ultimate good ole boy system has found a real home as a core element of the democrat philosophy. They see that in area after area, the principle of equal rights has been stacked against them—with the courts' approval.

I believe there is some strength to be gained from a united diversity, something the U.S. had at one time. But it has melted like snow in the spring with the democrat version of diversity. The democrat version of diversity will never yield a united diversity. The democrat diversity is largely government-mandated and government-enforced diversity; where it is unnatural. It is not the result of shared experiences, common interests, a common goal, mutual respect and admiration. Those types of things bring about a naturally occurring united diversity.

This version of diversity has become so pervasive to the democrat, it is accepted as a naturally occurring phenomenon. This is evident from the statements uttered by the Attorney General placed in office following the November 2008 elections. This guy is so clueless, having drunk his own propaganda, that he can't figure out the delta between eight-to-five, Monday-through-Friday diversity, and weekend diversity. Duh.

This democrat diversity enacted by revolutionary edict(s), not an evolutionary process, has thus brought with it wealth, power, and protection to millions of so-called minorities. They are protected from some of the realities of life that a non-minority must deal with, from incompetence on the job, to murder, to facing the truth. What apparently started out as an effort to ensure equal rights as stated in the Constitution, quickly became a system of preferential or unequal treatment. This clearly unconstitutional treatment has not only been permitted by a court system run amuck, it has been adopted by the courts. But as I have observed elsewhere in this document, a court that can legalize abortion can legalize anything.

One of the by-products of the democrat diversity is that it has created a large segment of the population that is showered with hundreds of public and private welfare programs, which provide material goodies far beyond the basic necessities of life. Humans, being what they are, have quickly perverted this largess into anything and everything. Democrats have trained this segment of the population, and many foreigners, to believe that these programs are womb to tomb entitlements (which is another word for rights). No, the reader will not find that in the Constitution, but once again the courts have placed their holy stamp of approval on it.

Far from rejecting this preferred treatment bestowed upon them by the government and the courts, the minorities have not only embraced it, they have come to believe it is their right. Even in the face of having condemned recently the practice when it was applied to others. Could it be viewed as retribution, not on the perceived perpetrators of this practice, but on the sons, grandsons, great-grandsons, great-great-grandsons, et cetera? Why, yes. It not only could, it is.

This is so politically incorrect, one can expect the brown-shirted politically correct police to be on the rampage, much as they were with the politically incorrect people in Adolf Hitler's day. For like their predecessors, the police are not backed by the law, but by fear. The modern day version of the brown shirts or the black-uniformed Gestapo, of course, cannot be found so dressed. They wear coats and ties, and are found on the most influential of the media propaganda outlets—TV. They are also found frequently at the head of charitable organizations, or ruling as professors at northeastern colleges. It is not unusual to find that many of these have never had to work for a living, yet they express their views as if they held the keys to the kingdom of knowledge.

Certainly the founding fathers never saw this coming. Big government and courts today have no hesitation imposing cost (taxes by another name) on the states or on the public, either by court decision or by legislation. It's bad enough that some outside agency can impose high-impact decisions or laws without the public's approval, but then they wash their hands of that impact. If big government's decisions or big courts' rulings have a financial impact on the states or the public, then, by golly, they should pay the cost in full. There are many such big government decisions or actions. A classic example is the school busing decree. This is very high cost, and it is endless.

Many of these actions are in effect retroactive laws, when something that was legal or accepted for generations becomes illegal or unacceptable all of the sudden. The courts or government just wash their hands of the subject, basically telling the affected folk, "Don't ask me how to carry out my ruling and don't expect me to pay for it. Just get it done!" Concerned citizens, almost all the wisdom of our Founding Fathers has been trashed by our present-day central government. They would not recognize the institutions, except for the titles!

EQUAL RIGHTS, NOT EQUAL ASSETS

Had today's typical democrats participated in the writing of the Constitution and the Bill of Rights, the documents would have never been finished, or would have emerged in a radically different form. As written, the documents guarantee equal rights, not equal income, houses, vehicles, property, et cetera, which is, of course, impossible. Democrats, however, want special rights and special economic privileges, even today. Somehow they appear not to get it when they are given special rights at the expense of another. The other person is then being denied equal rights. Actually, I believe they really do get it, but do not care. In fact, they rejoice in it. Likewise, taking away another's economic gains (as in via taxation) and giving it to others is basically government-sanctioned stealing. Actual equal economic status is impossible with a free people, and even if it were possible, nothing in the Constitution requires it or even allows it. Mississippi is usually characterized as the poorest of the poor states. Actually, all states in this country are rich when compared with most of the world.

TRUST

Motto for today's citizens: Trust no one.

Trust: An honorable word, a desired character trait, a code of conduct fundamental to our country since its founding—until recently. Its worth is priceless; it is a miracle word.

Trust in the people: Before the country settled for less than the best, I would have totally trusted the American public to be fully informed and armed with the truth on both sides of any question or on any public issue placed before them. No more.

Trust in the jury: Likewise, at one time I would have trusted an American jury with my life. No more.

Trust in our institutions?

1. Big business: At the peak of the American industrial age, which I will define as the mid-twentieth century, most of our large businesses were run by technocrats, as opposed to today's bean counters. I hold this shift from the engineer/scientist to the Harvard MBA responsible for most of our economic woes of today. But even these people had some help from our "friend," Uncle Sam. Not only has Uncle Sam spent money he didn't have for programs he didn't have to have, he has imposed laws, rules, regulations, and so on, on the American businessman, which have threatened his livelihood, while failing completely in oversight responsibilities where oversight was warranted.

2. Education system: Although as stated in the opening of this little message, there will always be exceptions and there will always be pockets of education excellence, the American public education system is in decay beyond repair. Sure it will continue to exist, but it is a dead duck as far as the average student is concerned. I attribute this to integration, lawyers, the courts, and even the educators themselves, as well as the teachers union. Their typical cry is always the same—send more money. That is a lie, for the data clearly show no causal relationship. Students' standardized tests have been watered

down several times, and still scores slide. As I drafted this little piece, there was an article in the paper that tests were once again under review to make them more "contemporary and progressive." That is liberal speak for *easier*. the new tests will probably ask such questions as, "Recite the words to rapper Joe's latest release." Now, how "contemporary and progressive" can one get? Before it was destroyed by the above mentioned parties, there was a time when the Mississippi school administrators provided an environment where the teachers could teach, and the teachers were competent to teach, and students received a good education.

How bad is it? When my granddaughter finished her last year in junior high, the school held an awards day, which my lovely wife and I attended. It was an awards day to beat any awards day previously attended. Perhaps two hundred awards or certificates (suitable for framing) were given. About thirty to thirty-five of these awards were given for being in the choir. It appeared as if any student that was breathing got an award (or two or three). As would be expected, the scholastic awards were last (and marginalized) in this melee. Upon inquiry, a teacher said to me, "You have to remember, many of these children have low self-esteem." My stars, many of them already have a natural talent for music. Would it not be better to teach them to excel in something called academics?

3. Our churches: Many church clergy and bishops do not preach the Word, except to the degree that they want to back up their secular message and causes. Many openly deny the scriptures and embrace conduct specifically condemned by the scriptures. Why don't they just leave the church to go deliver their message to the public? I have a feeling the reason that they stay with the church is they have a captive audience, and they like the perks and money. They also know that outside the church, there may be no one to listen to their rantings; and no money. Thus in almost every denomination, we have people leading the Christian churches who apparently do not believe significant parts of, or perhaps none of, the scriptures, yet call themselves Christian. Would you call BHO's former pastor (of 20 years) a Christian? I thought not.

4. Courts: I don't think so. The legal system has been amply covered elsewhere. Another failed institution. Actually,

it is easy to see why the BHO minority-staffed, democrat administration would want to try the Islamic terrorist in civilian court. For the past sixty or seventy years, the courts have handed the minorities their every wish on a silver platter. The courts have sacrificed their very reason for being, their honor, and respect at the minority altar. They have allowed clearly unconstitutional legislation, executive orders and regulations to stand throughout the country. The courts are a biased friend to the minorities, giving the minorities a huge edge in any question. Trial lawyers mostly vote democrat, as do minorities. With the judge, the lawyer, and his minority client singing out of the same song book, it's tough for any opponent not in the loop. It is probable that the guy that made the decision to try the Islamic terrorist in civilian court and his boss are both lawyers. Finally, many democrats are sympathetic to the Islamic terrorists, some even blaming *us* (Bush, Cheney, and people such as me) for the murders on 9/11. These people appear to be far left-wing loons. A jury in these times could easily free these terrorists.

5. Lawyers: If it involves money, beware. That brings me to fees. No legal fee should be set by another lawyer, i.e., a judge. Fees in this country are totally out of control and are obscene. But there are so many judges with so much money, politicians cater to them. Lawyers make up a good percent of federal and state legislatures. Any meaningful tort reform is almost impossible due to the opposition of lawyers. Trial lawyers are especially troubling. It appears they are so steeped in practicing deception, half-truths, and innuendo, they lose the ability to step back from the courtroom to reality. Lawyers are frequently executors of estates. Guess who gets first choice in picking off the low-hanging fruit? This could go on for months. Briefly, however, many lawyers from time to time need adult supervision.

6. Doctors: As a class, these people have my respect, although their fees have risen far beyond the cost of living rates. This, it is noted, is partially driven by lawyers and courts, resulting in astronomical malpractice insurance costs. Do they make mistakes? Are there all varieties of doctors out there, good and bad? You bet. They are a cross section just like the rest of us,

and that is why those well-intended people that worship those with the title *doctor* should not.

7. The dollar: Don't ever expect to hear the expression "sound as a dollar" again. The late, great, and wealthy United States of America woke up one day and found itself in the poorhouse. The country was not taken or driven there by outside forces. We did it all by ourselves. We collectively drove ourselves directly from a grand mansion to the poorhouse, driving a foreign car pulling a trailer of fifteen million illegal aliens (yes, I can call a pig a pig); and a growing five-generation welfare segment using foreign oil and gas, paid for with food stamps and overly generous welfare programs that are subsidized with foreign money; wearing foreign-made clothes, listening to ear-splitting, mind-deadening music on a foreign-made radio, many high on foreign or domestic drugs. Today we would probably stop by the local hospital emergency room to be treated for the common cold. And what else would one expect after watching endless hours of low-IQ-level programs on the primary propaganda agent of the latter half of the twentieth century and spilling over into the twenty-first century. Exactly what we get.

Essentially everyone present in this country, legal or illegal, is sucking on one or more of the governments' (at all levels) teats. Even I, as a retired person, draw Social Security, although I did pay into it my entire working life. I am not drawing it without at least having paid my dues.

Think about it, please. Millions upon millions of government employees or contractors, that range all the way from the president to congressmen to governors to healthcare workers to the military to teachers to utility workers to college presidents; (Note: In this state if one draws a government pension upon retirement, I consider them a government employee) countless government agencies; and Social Security recipients. (One does not have to be a retired person to draw Social Security today. It has become just another welfare program.)

Countless welfare programs

Grant receivers (again, thousands upon thousands) The states (all of them)

Some states, cities, or companies receiving "bailouts" Public servants pension/health programs (billions annually)

From all this, there is not one manufactured product that can be exported.

The thousands of Defense Department contractors are not listed above, as they at least produce a usable product, although they still have a huge teat to suck on.

The net result of all this sucking is to not only drain the original wealth bag, but to drain all the government printing presses, as well as all the foreign loans. This would have not been possible in 1955, simply because it was inconceivable. Of course, back then Social Security had not been turned into a welfare program. And neither the masses nor the government have the willpower to put the brakes on. In fact, they are still going in the opposite direction with the health care bank breaker.

Withholding freebies from a largely dependent, "victimized" population can only be done without their permission, for the government will never get their permission to reduce or eliminate their handouts.

There are layered and multiple taxes paid on everything, except possibly the air we breathe. If a person smokes, he pays a hefty cigarette tax, and then he pays a sales tax, which means he pays taxes on the cigarette taxes. If he has paid into the Social Security system as a worker, then when he retires he must pay income tax on his already earned pension.

8. Government: BHO said he was going to pay for health care by elimination of "waste, fraud, and abuse." That, I believe, is a lie. W, F & A are not three fat white guys, as depicted in a recent cartoon. W, F & A will be found to be centered right there in Washington, DC,, and Chicago, LA, NY, Boston, et cetera, for these are his constituents and he is not going to touch them. He and his fellow democrats are good at watching reality shows, but totally at a loss in participating in the one here and now on center stage.

Although the government has in place oversight agencies for banks, securities, etcetera, at a cost of billions of dollars you have seen that these oversight functions routinely fail, sometimes in catastrophic proportions.

Now the government is asking you to trust them on health care. As you read this, anyone that snickers is automatically pardoned.

Recently my grandson and his lovely bride applied as first-time home buyers for some type of government tax break, perhaps part of the stimulus package program. After a lengthy search, they found a small but decent house, settled with the owner for a price, made a down payment, paid the inspection fees, et cetera, and settled in for the government's red-tape machine to run its course. This process started about 1 September 2009. After waiting and waiting, anticipating a closure date anytime, they finally got a call. But it wasn't a closure date. It was a call telling them that the program in this area had been frozen because the loans were not in ratio. Now if you have an IQ over one hundred, you know what that means. They were told it might be three to six months before they got approval—if they got approval. And the government wants you to trust them.

9. The media: This could take a book; however, let's go for the short version. Like BHO, the media, way back to Uncle Walter but far, far worse, not only shapes the news that is reported, it fails completely to cover some stories that don't fit its political-correctness agenda. BHO excels in the same antics. A half-truth is a lie, misinformation is a lie, misguiding is a lie, promises not kept is a lie, passing oneself off as a moderate when one is a left-wing radical is a lie, withholding information is a lie (if the subject is not military or intelligence related). The media of today have lost their purpose. For some, trust in the media began to erode at an age of maturity, with Uncle Walter putting his spin on the day's events.

The sole purpose of the media is to report the news. I call it informing the public. If a given item is newsworthy, the media is obligated to report both sides, or even a third if necessary, to fully inform the public. Misleading news over the public airways is a crime. For papers, if not a crime, at least it is irresponsible, contemptible and poor business. Of course, democrats have already thrown out character as unimportant. For them, Bill and Hill were getting the job done and that was all that mattered.

Over the years the paper that is distributed in this area has had so many *New York Times* columns in it that if you give me a subject, I can tell you the precise thrust of the column with 100 percent accuracy, and even some of its contents.

10. Charity: But for whom? In a news report last fall, the 2007 financial report for a so-called charity organization in Mississippi indicated the organization took in $4,470,000.00. Of that, $172,810.00 was identified as going to charity, while $407,490.00 went to administrative expenses and $2,900,000.00 went to fund-raising expenses. What happened to the other $1,000,000.00 was not specified. The executive director of this outfit stated that the organization "works to promote arts and provide scholarships for college students." Right. It's not much consolation, but under state law at least 40 percent of the intake has to go to charity. That's still only $1,788,000.00 of the $4,470,000.00. Yet another derailed train. Please select your charity carefully, and beware. Many "charities" are funded by your state or federal governments.

11. Character: Madoff, AIG, WorldCom, Stanford, Fannie Mae, Bear-Stearns, Freddie Mac, Goldman Sachs, Chicago, Tyco, Lehman Bros., Merrill Lynch/Bank of America, ACORN, SEIU, John Adams(NOT the long gone former President), Scrushy/HealthSouth. Please don't link my name with any of this trash.

ANARCHY-LEFT-LIBERAL

It may appear to be a paradox, but not so. On one hand, the democrat appears to support anarchy—no rules, no constraints. I have my rights, and no one can tell me what to do. On the other hand, this element wants a government that will satisfy all their wants, and these wants are endless. Increasingly, governments and courts today are yielding to these block votes, and are giving unprecedented and special rights to these segments of the population who have some form of itch. It may be an abortion right, a special protection right, a special punishment right, a special voting right, a special health care right, or a financial support right, in a thousand forms. Tragically, the courts have supported or even lead in this unequal treatment of citizens.

Some of you may remember that it wasn't too long ago when abortion was considered murder and was illegal in the United States of America. What changed? Certainly not the act nor the Constitution. Both are precisely the same. What changed was the makeup of the Supreme Court and the mindset of some of the citizens of this country. Not an encouraging sign for a nation founded on a precisely written constitution. A court that can legalize abortion can legalize *anything!* And they will. Just stand by, for it is only a matter of time when everything will be legal except three things:

1. Christianity
2. Any of the principles laid down by the Founding Fathers
3. Traditional straight white male activities

In fact, we are well on our way there now.

Sarah Palin recounted a situation with her son in her book *Going Rogue*. Her seventeen-year-old son had been taken to the hospital emergency room for a dislocated shoulder. He wanted a drink of water, and the hospital refused to give it to him on the grounds that they could do nothing to him without his parents' permission. Now, make no mistake about it, the reason the hospital would not give the boy a drink of water was not they wanted to be unreasonable, but because they *live in fear* of being sued by some money-hungry lawyer looking to make a quick million. This idea of no drink of water without parental approval is contrasted with the fact that a thirteen-year-old female can get an abortion in that same hospital without even notification of her parents, let alone approval. In a court-ordered motion, this striking example demonstrates the lack of common sense, the lack of fairness, and the lack of a firm anchor (called the Constitution) by the courts, including especially the top court. Conversely, it presents the overwhelming argument that the courts have been and are engaged in a vast social engineering program that supports the liberal left. These courts need some adult supervision, which constitutionally should be provided by the other two branches of the government.

Once again, a court that can legalize abortion can (and will) legalize *anything*.

What some citizens appear to want is equality of all citizens, and in the interests of gaining that goal, they are perfectly willing to accept special considerations or privileges. Those particular people cry equality, but what they really want is ascendancy. They are assisted in countless ways by an unthinking court system and by a sympathetic government. Thomas Jefferson: "If we can but prevent the government from wasting the labors of the people, under the pretense of taking care of them, they must become happy." Clearly, the people are not happy.

PART III

POLITICAL PARTIES

Political parties are an unnecessary evil in our republic. Ditto for party line votes, either in our election or in a vote in Congress. An unthinking party line vote robs the citizens of the best candidate and the best congressional activity. Think about this carefully. First, the designated party candidate might be the only candidate put forth for that party, and he might have been selected by a bare majority of a group that has overriding selfish or vested interests and the loudest mouths. As recently as the fall of 2009, for example, the GOP supported a liberal female as the party candidate for an upstate New York district. It was such a poor choice, both the democrat and independent candidates were more conservative than the GOP-backed candidate. She was dead last in the polls, and at the last minute dropped out and endorsed the democrat, not the more conservative independent. So much for the political parties. It happens.

If this designated party candidate gets elected, he goes to Washington to vote the party line. That means that other (and perhaps better) laws are excluded because the party has made the choice for him, and all he has to do is vote "aye." It happens, folks. Although there are some in a political party who do not blindly follow party lines, many do, and they put a misguided party loyalty above the best for their constituents and for the country.

Although I mostly vote for Republican candidates, because their platform most closely follows my thinking, I consider myself a free-thinking independent and belong to no political party. I have made donations to a few democrats and many Republicans. There isn't a Republican who got my vote whom I didn't disagree with from time to time, because of a particular vote or action. Over the many years, however, it has been found that with exceptions, one could count on his fingers the very worst of the Republicans, are far better than the very best of the democrats. This is a reference point for the democrat of today, not the many revered democrats of old. At this writing, I cannot think of a single democrat platform plank worthy of support.

While political parties are not supported, if one is going to belong to a political party, he should be honest in his identification. There are some that identify with a party label, but their voting record puts them in the other party. The sensible choice for all citizens is to be independent. While their vote may not always turn out to be the best course, it lets them be honest. At the same time, it keeps them from doing something stupid, like voting for a crazy law because that is the party line. And yes, if there are going to be political parties, it is time to change the names. The Republican Party should be renamed the Tea Party and the Democrat Party should be renamed the Kool-Aid Party.

THE CENTRAL GOVERNMENT

The central government's task is to guide at the appropriate time and place, but not to run the show. A prime example is the old antitrust laws. When humans insist on being human, sometimes greed is the rule. When this is shown to be harmful to the citizens (not to *a* citizen), it is appropriate for the government to give guidance in the form of a law to prevent or curb this practice. Now, when a local businessman practices the same thing in a limited area, it is the place of competition to step in and correct that situation, not the federal government.

Why we need health care reform (but not the BHO type):

The local hospital is county-owned and operated. If someone needs emergency treatment or hospital care and is not insured or is unable to pay for those services, he is treated free. At one time in the hospital's budget planning, about 40 percent of patients was expected to be non-payers. Now that 40 percent is not covered by the population in general in the form of taxes, but is covered by those that have insurance or pay cash. Even though this hospital is supposed to be a non-profit organization; it does in fact make a profit. This profit is disposed of in many ways—exercise facilities, purchase of doctors practices, advertising, and buildings. Almost since it began in the 1960s, the local hospital has been building, building, and building and remodeling. Even though the local community is no longer a growth area, the hospital keeps building. One of the evils of this system is that for those people that have insurance, the insurance cost is about 40 percent above what it should be to cover their actual cost, since they are also covering the cost of the uninsured. That means that if the general population were taxed to cover the uninsured and non-payers, insurance rates would be cut almost in half. That, of course, means that more people could afford health insurance. That is the kind of health care reform we should be looking at.

A local city has a similar problem with its abuse of a gas franchise. This city has the natural gas franchise and sells gas to its citizens at a profit. This gas profit is then used to fund city expenses. This means those individuals with gas facilities in their homes subsidize those all-electric people in funding city expense. A proper use of this franchise by the city would be to sell its natural gas at cost and tax the general population for the funds to support the city expenses. That way, all citizens would pay a more equal share.

In both of these situations, the hospital abuse and the city abuse, probably the reason they do not tax the general population is that the larger property owners have more influence on the city and county officials, and they do not want to pay more taxes. A distant second reason is that it raises taxes in an already high tax environment. Besides being more equitable and fair to the people with health insurance and to the city's gas customers, the slight addition of taxes paid by the general population would be tax deductible. Not so with utility bills or hospital bills.

ENTITLEMENTS

The government has instituted an out of control and financially irresponsible "entitlement" program. No man enters this world with any more entitlement than a lion cub born in Africa. The world owes no one a living. All that aside, there are some situations where a civilized society should provide assistance to individual members of society (not an entire segment of society) based on their needs. Society is not obligated to help such people achieve par with the average member of society, however.

Except as above, entitlement comes from paying one's dues. Entitlement should be according to a person's contribution, not to put him on par with anyone else. When a worker pays his dues, he becomes entitled to a pension in his old age or upon disability. In the recent past, when some business executives have spent, given away, or lost employees' pensions, thus voiding those employees' entitled pension, simple jail time is not sufficient punishment. Even though most of these criminals somehow manage to hide and hold onto large sums of money, there should be no "minimum security detention center" haven for these lowlifes. No television, no special treatment, no civilian clothes--just life at hard labor. That way, someday in the distant future they may wake up and say to themselves, "What did I do and why did I do it? God forgive me for this horrible crime against so many innocent people." To which perhaps the Lord would respond, "I heard your prayer and you are forgiven. Now get back to work breaking up those big rocks." And that sounds fair to me. I would call it justice.

Welfare? *no.*

When my dad passed away at age fifty-seven, he left my mom with four children and a mortgage payment. Since he had worked most of his life as a government employee, Mom was denied Social Security and there was no government pension. Did she and the children have a "right" to some type of pension? Well, apparently she did not, since she did not get one. Faced with a stacked deck, did she wind up on welfare? No, not at all. Although she had never worked outside the home before, she took a part-time job as a crossing guard for a school. Rain, sun, snow, sleet, she was on the job, sometimes with a raging fever. She could not afford to miss a single day. Her income shortfall was covered by the older children that had left home. Small monthly checks were sent to ensure her necessities were met. She lived for almost forty years after my father's death. Did she ever hit the welfare rolls? No. Even in today's welfare state, if we had it to do over again, would we place her on the welfare rolls? Never.

THE WELFARE CLASS FARES WELL

A while back I stopped at a small family owned grocery store (not many of these survive) to pick up a couple of items for my lovely wife. In the checkout line in front of me there was a nicely dressed woman that paid for her groceries with an EBT card (food stamps). By the time she got her groceries loaded in her car I had checked out my two items and was outside. As I got in my truck I noticed her car – it was a 2009 luxury car. What happens in that other states I do not know, but in this state the welfare class apparently fares well.

As time goes, this country is gone from a society that could barely share enough with the poor to help them survive, to a society in which the politicians cannot give them enough; especially as it is someone else's money. In making this transition we have gone from a society which had poor people, but no welfare class to a society that has no poor people but a huge welfare class.

In the former time the nation was not hopelessly in debt; in fact it was rich, probably the or one of the wealthiest nations on the planet. The country has now 50 years later poured that wealth down the drain with little or nothing to show for it in the form of hardware or a more civilized, cultured, creative or educated society. That the government has burdened the next generation with a monumental debt does not appear to be a concern, based on voter data, to the welfare class. I suppose their rationale is "Hey, I'm going to be on the receiving end of the welfare state; someone else will be doing the paying off thing". Why else would they continue to vote for people that pander to their every wish. Who pays for welfare? Seems logical to say that anyone that pays taxes and is not on welfare pays for welfare. Yes, any one that pays taxes and is not on welfare, helps pay for the food stamps, the housing allowance, the telephone allowance, the power allowance, that aid – to – dependent children and on and on and on. Specifically, the guy with a young family of perhaps a wife and a child or two, struggling to get started, maybe driving a 10 year old car is helping to pay for the food stamps for the woman driving the 2009 luxury car. Go back and read that last sentence again, please for I want you to understand exactly who pays for welfare. It is not just the rich people that pay for welfare – we ALL pay if we work and are not on welfare. It matters not to the government that this young man may be struggling to pay his own bills; the government is going to give priority to the welfare recipient for that is a vote in the bank to a democrat.

A BETTER WAY

Most democrats wear blinders. Once they target an area that they think needs their attention, they say, "Let's fix it, and let's fix it this specific way." And that way is usually via some government giveaway program.

But would it not be better, for instance, to develop our manufacturing base, so that *anyone* who wanted a decent job could get it? That is a much better option than some giveaway program that only provides food stamps (now called EBT cards), or welfare, other giveaway programs that do not yield any positive economic or personal benefits. Of course, some folk apparently not only live pretty well off food stamps and welfare, but they are completely satisfied with that situation. Would it not be better and cheaper to provide the education community with the environment to teach students year by year, so that they learn the material and are passed to the next grade on merit, rather than passing them on because "to fail them and keep them in the same grade would damage their ego"? As it is now, in the schools where students are passed out of school on an "ego" basis, someone had the idea to provide free government remedial education. Failure piled on top of failure. Education of our children is far too important for teachers to fail to take some student to task for disrupting a class, or for tolerating an incompetent teacher due to an affirmative action program or some such other political-correctness ploy. Playing hardball with education impediments would send a message quickly, and we would return to the days when it was understood by all that bad behavior or incompetence just would not be tolerated. Now that may twist the tails of a few people, but think of the benefit to the students that want to or at least are willing to get an education. A disruptive student or incompetent teacher should be a zero tolerance item, just as much as a weapon on school property. The effect of a disruptive student or incompetent teacher is like a weapon on campus, only instead of killing the body, it kills the mind.

OPENNESS

The American people traditionally have loved a guy such as Mike Huckabee – straightforward, an open book, what you see is what you get, knowledgeable, even blunt! Of course, the modern day media prefer the dodger (in at least one case, a draft dodger) such as Carter, Clinton and BHO. When my lovely wife made the comment recently that she thought Huckabee would make a good president, I responded with the media would never allow it, and the same can be said of Sarah. They are already working on her in a frenzy. Mitt Romney was somewhat that type when he ran for the presidency in 2008. His failing was that he had some attractive characteristics like Huckabee, but the media would have none of that. The media would say that such men are a little rough around the edges and they might be a little abrasive to some people! And of course they would be correct, but that to me is a plus, not a negative. The media prefer the rounded, smooth surface that slides along on its belly.

NEWSPAPERS/TELEVISION

Newspapers are not what they were. Once there were hundreds, if not thousands of newspapers, from tiny to the big city giants. Most were local and privately owned. From this fertile field, the American public enjoyed a mostly factual account of the news and the local editors' views on local, state, and federal politicians. Should the editor be a tad off the mark, it was a local matter. At any rate, the public got an honest, straight-up diversity of opinion. The papers I read today that are locally available are part of a conglomerate that spits out a party line. For serious politics, one locally available paper almost exclusively uses *New York Times* columnists for indoctrination of the local populace. No diversity of opinion here; liberal or radical to a column. That these papers appear to be a dying breed will bring no tear to these eyes. Compared with the power of television, newspapers are not a force, at any rate.

MASS MEDIA MOTOR MOUTHS

One of the reasons so many Americans love Sarah Palin is that no matter what she does, skeet shooting, fishing in the frigid waters off Alaska, mothering or campaigning she comes across as 100% genuine and 100% percent feminine. Where in Hillary or Michele can one find anything feminine or genuine. One will never figure that out from the portrayals of the mass Media Motor Mouths. The mass media specializes in putting the information they want and only that information in the minds of the American citizens, information framed to yield a particular mindset in the individual. They look at a guy like Dan Quayle, who as earlier stated, appeared to me to be a steady, sensible man, or to Sarah Palin or to Joe the plumber or Jess Brasher and say to themselves; "Uh, oh, I don't believe our propaganda is going to fall on receptive ears; he looks like one of those that want to think for themselves. We better take this guy down." To them the daily "news" reports are merely another opportunity for them to get their own single purpose propaganda to the public. To these people it is not about getting the most complete and accurate objective information to the public, it's getting their version of the events or subjects to the public which are directed to serve their own purposes. If the situation being reported in any way it lends itself to a liberal or radical slant it will be passed to the public in that manner.

WHAT COULD HAVE BEEN

That sets the stage for what could have been and still can be the most effective tool for *good change* this country has ever witnessed—television. Of course, after years of living in a garbage pit, it would require a lot of backing and filling to purge this garbage from the masses. Still, the power of the television is such that it could be done.

Think of it—taking all those low-IQ sitcoms and replacing them with mature adults conducting themselves in a civilized society. Ditch all the Star Wars stuff, or at least confine it to one "comic book hour" and replace the rest of it with education programming. Trash all the sex shows and implement programs that show constructive, responsible behavior. Teaching a ten-year-old to try to behave like a twenty-year-old is not constructive. Television routinely bestows on a five-year-old the wisdom to put down any adult white straight male.

The possibilities are endless—reduction of crime, vastly improved education, respect of others and their rights, no more road rage, no more mass murders, responsibility by all members of society. We would have a vastly more civilized society. Perhaps the country could even return to the days when one could leave his house unlocked, when children in the second grade didn't cuss like sailors, when there was no road rage, when greed was not the driving force, and when justice was as Aristotle defined it. Could we go back to a day when the clothes we wore might be thin and patched, but they were clean and pressed; and perhaps when people dressed as young adults or adults, rather than clowns? Could we go back to great music and entertaining movies? Could we go back to a time when any able-bodied man worked to pay his way? Could we go back to a civil society? Could we go back to greatness? Could we go back to wealth created by manufacturing, rather than false wealth created by government printing presses? Could we go back to a time when a reality show was life all around you?

THE UNQUESTIONED INFLUENCE

Mostly television teaches the masses trashy, crude, offensive, and criminal conduct. The media, as well as anyone with a triple digit IQ, know of television's huge influence on the masses and their conduct, actions, and thoughts. But when an individual acts outrageously or with criminal conduct, the media, backed up by the liberal courts, deny that they are in any way responsible. Now the media takes their stand because there are bucks on the table, and bucks on the table trumps their concern for some guy rubbing out a person or two. They and the courts wash their hands of the whole episode. The courts, however, come from a different direction, about which I can only speculate. As put forth in another section of this book, the courts are rightly concerned with the issue of free speech. Therefore, they allow almost any form of conduct, actions, and expressions. There are highly selected areas where they limit freedom of speech, usually, but not always, in an area of safety. The courts, however, utterly fail to bring justice (better known as fairness) into the argument. If the courts are going to allow extreme interpretations of freedom of expression, conduct, et cetera, although not necessarily speech, then they should also allow generous recoveries for offended parties. It is as simple as that. The reason for their outrageous conduct is found in the left's focus on rights (freedom of speech) and total disregard for responsibility (recovery for abuse of that right).

That the media and the courts are out in left field is an open and shut case, when one considers that companies, individuals, and even government agencies shell out millions of dollars for a few seconds of advertising on television. Politicians, political organizations, and, heaven forbid, even judges running for office or reelection use television ads to influence the masses. So if it works, and it does, how can the media and the courts claim it does not work, when some guy act in a criminal and possibly deadly way? With a straight face yet. Duh! Actually, just another case of the courts lost and wandering in the wilderness with no star (or document) to guide them.

BUSINESS, NOT FUN AND GAMES

Democrats are not progressive, according to Webster's. The democrats are and have been taking the country down the road of lowest common denominator, a dumbed-down society, uneducated, irresponsible, welfare zombies, out of control debt, out of control trade deficits, out of control entitlements, out of control government. This country, any country, can only tolerate so much of that poison, and then it will die. For a country to be successful, it must have an educated, mature, industrious population. America is rapidly phasing from the latter to the former. And for some strange reason, the democrats revel in it.

Long before cigarette manufacturing companies were required to put warning labels on cigarette packages, it was common knowledge that cigarettes were not healthy. In the early 1940s, there was a song that went "Smoke, smoke, smoke that cigarette, smoke yourself to death," or close to that. It was routine to refer to a cigarette as "another nail in your coffin." No responsibility for a smoker's own choices. Were I on a jury, a lawyer would have a very difficult time getting me to hold a cigarette company wholly responsible. Who really wins here? The lawyers, while the smokers get the crumbs. Personal responsibility; you can't live without it—and be successful.

As this piece is written, the democrats are in Washington scratching their heads and wringing their hands over the unemployment level and how to create jobs. In fact the BHO administration doesn't have a clue as to how to generate jobs, real honest-to-goodness jobs. They have not one specific plan. Their standard proposal is to throw money in that direction and wish something will happen, when the obvious answer is at the end of their big noses. It is simple: *Buy American, stupid!*

DO NOT READ THIS UNLESS YOU APPRECIATE TRUTH

This is so, so politically incorrect—dare anyone say it. The decline of America is almost exclusively attributed to the liberal fixation on minorities and to an unbalanced concern for rights, with essentially no regard to responsibilities or duties. As a young adult, I remember hearing that integrated schools would result in the minorities being lifted up to the performance level of the white students. Of course, in those days there was, for all practical purposes, one minority. The homosexuals were still in the closets, and the others classified as minorities today were not recognized as such, except in the nightmares of the liberals. Integration of the schools has resulted in destruction of our once great academic institutions, from grades one to twelve schools, to colleges and graduate schools. And basically the once great system did it on a shoestring, not on unlimited funding. Education is prominent in the decline of the great American empire. Extrapolate that to morals, violence, craftsmanship, drugs, crime, banking/ finance/home mortgages, safety/national security, welfare, entitlements, government, and one can see why the United States of America is no longer king of the hill. It may not even be *on* the hill much longer.

The United States, given today's environment, can never compete in the manufacturing sector with, for example, Japan. Think about it for a minute and you will come up with not one or two, but a dozen reasons why.

To be completely honest, the liberals, with their fixation on minorities and rights, could not have pulled off all that they have without the help of their lawyers, the courts, and the media. Sad.

AFFIRMATIVE ACTION: SPECIAL AND UNEQUAL TREATMENT

Prior to my retirement, every year a member of a minority (actually a double minority), come to me with a spreadsheet of my employees. She would proceed down the list, saying something like this: "I see you only have one minority in this category, when based on local population ratios you should have X. What is your goal for next year to correct this disparity?" True story. Can you imagine the damage done to a company, a profession, a government agency, a society, not to mention the damage done to the displaced but more qualified person, when this accumulated effect impacts it? A habitual practice such as this yields exactly what this country has today—economic meltdown, poor education, poor performance, and national decline. Don't believe it? Well, according to media reports, the best cars built today in the U.S. are foreign cars built under the management of a foreign company. Case closed.

All this, mind you, while a contract with another arm of the government promised my company was an "equal opportunity employer." Of course, that wasn't real either, for you were expected to give certain people the benefit of special treatment to get them on the payroll. In my entire working career, there was only one situation when I was able to stiff - arm these Gestapo tactics. For one program, a special training class with written and oral examinations was required by yet another arm of the central government. In the early days of this government fiasco, it was established that to pass the course successfully—and the passing grade was 75, not 50—applicants were required to attain at least a minimum score on a pre-employment exam, Due to attrition and expanded work, a new class of about thirty to thirty-five applicants was needed. I assumed the pre-employment screening examination was still in place. However, much to my chagrin, at the end of the first three weeks, only five or six of the original applicants were still in the class. It was determined later that the original employee requisition was filled with people who had apparently been swept up off the streets by the Employment Office and shipped to me without the pre-employment examinations. Of course, the class had to be restarted. Think of the waste, should one multiply that by each company, each state, and the nation. Had I yielded, think of the negative impact on the program.

The truth is, no one really knows what negative impact all this failure to use the best person for each and every task has had on our country, but it has to be huge.

AND FINALLY

Things were really jumping out of the cauldron in the fall of 2009, as the newly elected radicals of the administration attempted to push their revolutionary agenda and nail shut the coffin lid on the late great United States of America.

In rapid-fire sequence, it was decided that the Muslim that killed thirteen people in the Fort Hood terrorist attack would be tried in a military court. Now this guy was born in the U.S., although I doubt that he was ever an American. Are you still with me? If so, read the following carefully and slowly. Within days of the above announcement, the attorney general (mentioned earlier in this transcript as a prominent low IQ possibility) announced that some of the top Muslim terrorists in the 9/11 disaster would be brought to New York and tried in a civilian court. This ties in with the possibility of bringing many more terrorists to the U.S. and giving them civilian court trials. Some of this was because BHO wanted to shut down Gitmo by January 2010—a purely arbitrary date. These are foreign terrorists being given the full rights of American citizens in a legal system that is infamous for its failures. The reader may want to read that again. As usual, BHO does not have the moxie to reel in this left-wing radical dream. The reason for this I would place in one of three categories—ignorance, low IQ, or a sympathetic attitude toward the terrorists, since they are much more likely to get off scot free in a civilian court. Some have heard the old saying of the inmates being placed in charge of the asylum. Well, it appears the U.S. has arrived: the inmates are in charge.

To give the country's masses that voted BHO into office some credit, one has to say that were it not for the mass media's failure to tell the public what this guy really stood for—revolution—he probably would not be in office today. Certainly had they known in November 2008 what they know in November 2009, BHO would never have been elected.

THE WRECKERS

Who and where are the culprits that have taken this once great country from the wealthiest, most powerful, most respected, and most admired country in the world, to the ranks of a banana republic? They are listed below, and they are located right here inside our borders. It's humiliating and embarrassing. However, some out there are, no doubt, celebrating our fall from greatness. Regardless, if there is any cause to celebrate, it can only be in the fact that we shot ourselves in the foot. No outside power could do it. Rome decayed in similar fashion.

1. The court judges are identified as the number one culprit, because today the judiciary is clearly the most powerful branch of the federal government; it is the leading activist; and it has discarded the Constitution, except as it suits its social agenda. None of the above was or is authorized by the Founding Fathers in the Constitution or in subsequent amendments. They are in chaotic free fall. The courts and judges, in particular the highest court judges, have discarded the Constitution and assumed the role of social engineers, legislators, and executives; court conduct never envisioned by the founders of the country. Once again, a court that can legalize abortion can legalize anything, and sooner or later it will. Next will be marijuana.

THE GUILTY PARTY

Amendment I:

Congress shall make no law respecting an establishment of religion, or prohibiting the free exercise thereof; or abridging the freedom of speech, or of the press; or the right of the people peaceably to assemble, and to petition the Government for a redress of grievances.

Amendment XIV:

No State shall make or enforce any law which shall abridge the privileges or immunities of citizens of the United States; nor shall any State deprive any person of life, liberty, or property, without due process of law; nor deny to any person within its jurisdiction the equal protection of the laws.

The above words are from two amendments to the Constitution. Today we are so submersed in the "interpretation" of the Constitution that almost no one thinks to read the *words* of the Constitution. Read the above articles slowly, word by word, and let them soak in thoroughly. Did you notice that Amendment I starts out "Congress shall ..." and Amendment XIV starts out "No state shall ..."? Does that mean that for Amendment I, the courts are permitted to; or for Amendment XIV, the courts are permitted to? Certainly not. In both these instances, it is the courts, not Congress and not the states, that abridge the citizen's rights. I am of the opinion that the reason the courts were not specifically named, as were Congress and the States, is that in their deliberations, the authors of the Constitution never envisioned that the arbiter of justice would be the guilty party in these violations of the Constitution. Wouldn't one expect the Congress, the states, or the president to step in and take control of these courts gone wild? They are apparently intimidated by the phrase, "We are a nation of laws," and do not want to be accused of breaking the law. But what if the supreme law, that is, the Constitution, is routinely broken by the very body that is supposed to be the source of supreme justice and above reproach? It is time for Congress, the states, and the president to bite the bullet and restore the balance of power among the three branches of government. Actually, it is past time. These lawyers and judges need some serious adult supervision.

When the courts transition from a simple ruling of constitutional or unconstitutional to a decision that expresses their opinion of what direction the parties should take, they are in fact performing a legislative and, by default, an executive function. This is the path that has led to an 800 pound gorilla in the midst of the three branches of government with their checks and balances. Again, this situation begs for correction if we are going to survive as a republic. Had the courts remained true to their assigned task, some of the following "wreckers" would not be an issue. Fairness and justice--courts, that is your assignment. Constitutional or unconstitutional--courts, that is your assignment. Nothing more; nothing less.

2. The Federal Government. This could take a seven-volume book, but I will be a little briefer. Aside from the massive, wasteful, and fraudulent welfare programs, any government that would order the bankers of this country to make housing loans to people that they know cannot afford them is not just irresponsible, it is stupid. It is idiotic. It is crazy. Aside from those characteristics, the government is supposed to regulate banks. Their order clearly directed banks in detail about how to do their business. Not only is it stupid, it is illegal. Make no bones about it. This entire bank mess originated as a method to provide minorities with another welfare freebie. The government welfare system is not the one portrayed in the media, as taking from the rich and giving to the poor. No, this welfare system takes from the entire working class. Any and all that pay Social Security taxes pay into the welfare system. Government stealing sanctioned by the courts because it fits their own social engineering program.

3. Lawyers. The proliferation of lawyers is primarily due to their ability to get rich quick. One big case is like winning the lottery. If these people were paid in some sane or rational manner, they would not be as thick as fleas. Should a man win a case, he is not paid by the loser. The lawyer is paid. The lawyer keeps what he wants and gives the rest to the winning party, who actually is not the winning party. The lawyer is.

4. Television. Oh, what might have been. What could have been The greatest instrument for advancement of civilization known to man, instead is one of the greatest, if not the greatest, waste of man's time... As if that were not enough, this time waster

dumbs down to the lowest common denominator almost every single program it touches.

5. Minorities. These special interest groups are pampered by the courts, judges, the media, and the government. Although it is patently unconstitutional (for it violates the equal rights clause), they are routinely given special rights by the judges and the government.

6. Immigration. Uncontrolled immigration has helped change the national character in a negative manner. Actually, to the point that the old country no longer exists.

7. Welfare. Sometimes called entitlements. None of us is entitled to anything except freedom and the rights enumerated by the Founding Fathers. No one in this once great country knows the true cost of the countless public and private welfare program; and now the government is desperately attempting to crank out the granddaddy of them all—health care.

8. Integration of the schools or, at a minimum, the manner in which it has and is being managed.

9. Political correctness. This evil conduct is simply a democrat device to intimidate you and deny you freedom of speech.

10. Unions. Greed and power seasoned with stupidity is a sure recipe for disaster every time. These people have crippled, and actually killed in some cases, American private industry wherever they are found. The only reason they haven't killed the public sectors is, the public sector just sucks the extra cost out of the deep pockets of the taxpayer.

11. Movies. Guys in serious need of a lengthy stay at the rehab house are making propaganda movies that spin a social message designed to program the masses into accepting his weird views.

12. Us. Some of us have seen, even anticipated, some of the crimes against our country, and we blinked, just as did many citizens in Nazi Germany in the 1930s. Before the disaster was brought upon us, we had time to act, but we failed. We allowed intimidation; fear of backlash; fear of being labeled non-progressive, or a reactionary, or a redneck; or disciplinary action on the job to keep us from acting or speaking. Yes, we were denied free speech.

13. Imports/Exports. It is a classic scenario. The door is cracked

just barely, and then a small flow becomes a stream, and gradually the stream becomes a flood. This is the story of American industry and foreign industry since World War II. In our sympathy and generosity to a struggling world, the United States gradually started importing some of Europe's products; and from one or two Volkswagens, we have graduated to millions of foreign cars. Hundreds of other products—electronics, clothing, utensils, ceramics, toys, linens, furniture, tools, heavy equipment, parts, even down to pen and paper—we have bought from these foreign countries, neglecting our manufacturing sectors to the point that the U.S. is not just broke, it is hopelessly in debt. We do not even own our own country. Although this is the last of the thirteen wreckers, it is not the least important by a long shot. Economically, the import sector, along with the welfare state created for the minorities, have destroyed our wealth. Further, I see no redemption until the rest of the world refuses to take worthless money, and we are forced to return to work in rebuilding our factories.

One can envision a United States neutered by foreigners, with countless factions making the country powerless to defend its own freedom, and the populace that made up the Greatest Generation and its descendants enslaved by a coalition of minorities. The white left radical who led the way in bringing that day about need take no comfort in this, for the minorities will no longer need him, and he will be discarded like a used soda can.

He can also envision an imploding economy, with the number of people willing to work unable to sustain the welfare payments of those who are unwilling to work; or if they are willing, are not capable of industriousness or creative and inventive work. Exports cease for all practical purposes, and because there are no factories left, everything is imported. A loaf of bread tops out at $3,000.00. Get the picture?

NOT CONSTITUTIONAL, NOT JUSTICE, NOT FAIR

That the courts have trashed the constitution can be clearly exposed by simply highlighting six topics:

1. Religion: The constitution says "Congress shall make no law respecting an establishment of religion..."

The courts have strayed from that simple, clear and precise statement to the other end of the world. It has ignored the first word "Congress" and addressed down to the level of a single citizen - a single citizen. It is gone around the world and lost the words... "respecting an establishment of (a national) religion." The courts have set themselves up to safeguard a fuzzy indeterminate - separation of church and state. This gigantic breach of the constitution by the courts is led to the exclusion of even the shadow of the word "God" from schools and many public places. The vast majority of Americans not only see nothing bad about the children singing "God Bless America" they see it is good. The constitution further states... "Or prohibiting the free exercise thereof..." It is only necessary to point out that when the courts by edict imposed silence in schools, public places, etc. it did exactly that.

Concerning religion, it is my opinion that the American public has much, much more to fear from a judicial dictatorship than from a theocracy - the former being a reality, the latter only a fantasy nightmare in the mindset of the liberal. Waving the red herring flag of theocracy is a method used by the liberals to achieve their purposes of a godless nation. This part of the constitution and its mismanagement by the court is a classic example of how the courts have come to trash the constitution to serve their own prejudices. It also renders null and void one of the fundamental foundations of the republic.

The original deviation from the words in the constitution is pronounced by some judge or some court and it is accepted without challenge. There is no appeal process for the "Supreme" court - only in theory by the other two branches of the central government; and we have already seen that just doesn't work for setting judges. Once the door is open, and even if it takes a magnifying glass to see crack, the inevitable follows. From that crack the flood gates open and some Federal judge finds himself edicting that little 6 year old Mary Jane can't take her lunch box to school because it has the word God on it somewhere. The courts are so wrapped up in their own prejudices they utterly fail to see that their own intrusiveness into the everyday life of the average American Citizen binds them in legal chains and they become slaves to an out-of- control court system.

I suspect that the only reason the "Supreme" court has not forbidden the words "In God we Trust" on our coins and paper money by court edict is that the constitution clearly gives Congress the power to "coin money". A direct challenge to supposedly an equal may be met with a chain saw. But in fact just such a confrontation is exactly what is not only due but past due. The Supreme Court must be brought to heel.

Hold on a second - did we not start out with something about "establishing a national religion". Are we not a million miles from that; why yes we are. When the court adopts an attitude on any specific of the constitution that any deviation, (no matter how small) is acceptable, it will always find itself dealing with a million people with a million combinations of issues which the court is helpless to deal with without contradicting itself daily and it does. Once the line is breached it is easy to expand the breach. Citizens are promised freedom of religion; not freedom from religion.

While the courts do not require that you show respect for the national flag or flag ceremonies it as clearly understood that you will show them respect every time they enter the courtroom by all standing. The courts are clearly unable to examine themselves on such issues as contradictions and/or hypocrisy. In my day respect was a treasure that was earned, not bestowed. When you were in school did Joe show any outward sign of great wisdom. I thought not, me either. Yet when Joe passes through a set of goal posts he may be vested with the word judge. Does that make Joe any more wise-- no, of course not. Now in the course of time if Joe does show signs of wisdom, knowledge, intelligence and maturity then he will have earned my respect. Not a day before. We should have faced the reality of today long ago and done away with that outdated habit of standing when a judge enters a room.

How far have we gone the other side of reason, intelligence, maturity and wisdom. It is my understanding that recently a school official refused to permit small (4"x8") copies of the Declaration of Independence and the Constitution of the United States to be passed out to students at the school. The copies were free. Do you not yet believe the courts are in free fall. The courts pursuit of a "separation of church and state" is therefore in large part responsible for the moral decline of this once great country.

In summary, all of the court decisions based on a theory of separation of church and state, therefore not the constitution, are thus invalid and citizens are not required to observe them and officials are not obligated to enforce them.

2. Abortion: If possible this stinks worse than the prior scenario. I cannot find this subject addressed in the constitution. Indirectly it is addressed in the Declaration of Independence where it states: "We hold these truths to be self - evident, that all men are <u>created equal</u>, that they are endowed by their <u>Creator</u> with certain unalienable rights, that among these are <u>Life</u>, Liberty and the pursuit of Happiness. There is a second document that deals with the issue of life and death. Is it possible that the Supreme Court would stoop to give any credibility to the Biblical Ten Commandments. Although the Ten Commandments are carved in stone on the building that houses the Supreme Court, the court fails to give them any merits in their pronouncements. To the present day court these carved in stone words appear to be something which they are intellectually unable to deal with, so they just quietly ignore it. Neither of these references are in the constitution so where does the Supreme Court get his authority for issuing edicts relative to abortion. The constitution was not written over night, it was not written by just one man, it was not written by illiterate men. The words, the sentences, the paragraphs and the entire document was carefully and thoroughly crafted. The United States Supreme Court alone is guilty of its destruction by

routinely ignoring the clearly written words of the constitution. The Supreme Court in mass should be impeached or if that is not possible simply allow them to die off and appoint no new justices. The country would be better off.

One Life - conception to death

There are those that would debate when is a baby a baby and/or when does life begin. Although this topic has been debated on and on and could be debated on and on, because the parties involved in the debate have an answer to the question up front and they want the debate (?) to come out to support their position.

Actually I do not see much to debate. Only life begets life. The dead do not reproduce. Therefore to originate a new (and eventually) an independent life, a live male must furnish an alive contribution (sperm) to a live female, alive component, (egg). This is called conception and it is impossible to accomplish between two females or between two males. Therefore one can see that only life begets life and one can readily see that it can only come about with the male contribution and a female contribution. Simple, precise and perfect in its intended purpose.

With that background one can readily see that for a human as well as other animals a new life began at the moment of conception. Now at that moment the new life does not appear as it will in 80 years, in 40 years, in 20 years, in 10 years, in 5 years, in 2 1/2 years, in 9 months or even in 4 1/2 months; but it will be a continuous life, assuming it is not murdered, or cut short by accident and disease. Therefore at conception a new and different individual is; let's repeat that; at conception a new and different individual IS. Assuming that individual continues to live to later stages it will become a baby (living on 'its' own systems), a little boy (or girl), a lad (or lass), a young man (or young lady), an adult male (or adult female), a middle aged man (or middle aged lady) and eventually an old man (or old lady). Now what is there to debate? Looks pretty simple and straightforward: life, a new individual, begins at the moment of conception unless aborted by some act, action or disease and this individual will live out its years in a state of progression. External to the womb this individual life is in a continuing state of change, the same as in the womb - a continuing state of change. NOTHING in the changing process either in the womb or out of the womb makes this life less of a life than it was the instance before, the day before or the year before. The only thing to debate is what is there to debate about something so obvious. Again a court that can legalize abortion can and will legalize ANYTHING. Shame, shame on us all. Shame on the courts for its decision. Shame on the Congress for they are supposed to be a check and balance on a court in rebellion. Shame on the office of the president for he is also charged as a check and balance for a court that has not only discarded of the constitution; it has discarded justice. And shame on us - the citizens - for allowing these politicians to get by with murder. Actually with only 6 million kills to his credit, Adolf Hitler was a piker compared to abortion when it comes to mass murder.

This is another case where a 150-170 year old fact was overturned by a social engineering minded court. Since I am unable to find the issue addressed in the constitution the court has not only trashed the constitution; it has trashed justice.

According to Webster:

Abortion: premature expulsion of a <u>fetus</u> that *it does not live*

Fetus: the unborn young of an animal or man, the offspring in the womb from the fourth month and until birth.

Offspring: a child or children; progeny, young.

Progeny: children; offspring

In summary, since there is nothing in the United States constitution to support this decision by the Court one may argue whether it is constitutional or not literally. However in the historical sanctity of life sense of this country, in the words of the Declaration of Independence, in the words of the Ten Commandments, in common sense and in a supposedly civilized country legalized abortion is not only unthinkable it is in violation of human decency and dignity. This decision by the court is thus void.

2. Equal protection of the laws: This topic was discussed elsewhere in this

document; however let me focus on what I consider open and shut case of tossing the constitution out the window. As in the issue of... "an establishment of (a national) religion..."Once a single judge has crossed the line without rebuttal, from that single case the tentacles spread like a cancer and in a flash the courts have ignored the reality of what it has just done. How can they close their eye and mind to the blatant violation of the document their whole purpose of which is to safeguard. But still they blindly charge ahead even at the obvious violation. Why? I can only speculate that the courts misplaced its priorities by placing the wants of a single individual ahead of the constitution and the rights of another individual. I mean a denial of equal protection of the laws. And there is no question of the validity of the issue and the dictatorship of the courts.

Anytime the court orders or allows preferential treatment of an individual or segment of the population it is denying equal protection to another individual or population segment. Now they may believe they have a valid reason for denying some citizens "equal protection" and thus violating the constitution. But that is not their responsibility or their authority. They are charged with safeguarding the constitution not to violate it, not to legislate, not to execute. It gets worse, once again when they cross the line it becomes easier and easier, it embroils more and more individual and more and more situations. Who knows, if the court had not blindly jumped in to violate the more qualified white males' rights to medical school entry the Congress may have had the wisdom to buy another chair for the medical school. And that is a more sensible solution. But the mindset of the courts on this issue is what results in a person coming to your office and asking what are you doing to get your ratios proper. This amounts not only to trashing the constitution but to rubbing your nose in their arrogance and waste. Affirmative action, preferential treatment etc.-all are totally unconstitutional.

In summary all decisions by the courts in requiring or permitting such things as affirmative action, preferential treatment of any individual or segment of the population are void because they are unconstitutional and need not be honored by the American citizen or entities.

4. The Right to Bear Arms: The words in the constitution read as
   follows: "...The right of the people to keep and bear arms shall not
   be infringed." Now these words need no genius to say what they
   mean-they are very simple and clear. (Although I'm sure Clinton
   could find a way to distort them.) They clearly say you have a
   right to own a firearm. So what is there to debate? But wait, the
   constitution goes further, much further. The constitution clearly
   says you have a right to have and bear a firearm. BUT it also
   states that right shall not be infringed. Those words mean that
   those locales, those cities such as Chicago and the District of
   Columbia cannot place any restriction on your ownership. They
   cannot require a license, they cannot require a registration, they
   cannot impose a single restriction on your ownership. That is what
   "infringement" means. So how do the courts justify their tolerance
   of these blatant violations of the constitution by cities. It's easy, since
   they long ago trashed the constitution and some court members
   are only interested in their social agenda they simply ignore the
   clear written word. For such an issue where the constitution is so
   clear why would the court even consider hearing a case challenging
   the right of ownership. Are they afraid of offending the liberals.
   Are they hoping to hear some unique, off the wall argument that
   may change the course of history in a dramatic way. If not, why?
   Why not refuse to hear such a challenge; why not save court
   time and the taxpayer money with a simple NO. The reason is,
   of course, is that a social engineering court is more interested is
   reshaping <u>society</u> than it is in <u>protecting</u> the constitution. While
   one may feel that ownership of a high powered assault weapon
   may be questionable that is not what the constitution words say.
   They say the right shall not be infringed. Should the court impose
   such a restriction in violation of the constitution tomorrow it will
   go further, and so on and on and until they reach the point that
   the court itself has denied and infringed the citizen's right to gun
   ownership. On some constitutional issues we are there today.
   In summary, any decision by the courts or any ordinance
   or law by a state or local unit which in anyway prohibits
   or regulates gun ownership is unconstitutional since such
   "infringes" upon the right to bear arms. Any required license,
   registration, records of possession, etc. are unconstitutional
   and therefore cannot be required of any American citizen.

5. Freedom of speech: In large and small ways the courts are the guilty party in trashing this article of the constitution for it is their rulings that prohibit Americans from saying certain words, from singing certain songs and for speaking out on certain issues. Although one may be allowed to do these things in certain locations or in ones home, please do not be so naive as to believe for a single minute that you will be allowed to do so even in these sanctuaries of today by some court edict of tomorrow. Again once the line of the constitution is breached the courts CAN and WILL find it easier and easier to go a little further, then a little more, then a little more, etc.

True Americans have long prided themselves as a model of a nation of laws and most even today are not aware that we have gradually graduated from a nation of laws to a national judicial dictatorship with some laws imposed by the courts, not by Congress as specified in the constitution. In other sections of this book one will find an extensive discussion of the evils of politically correct speech. Politically correct speech is of course a limitation on your speech therefore a form of denial of freedom of speech. This modern day evil to my knowledge is not a baby birthed by the courts but of the liberals and/or minorities. It is made possible as an effective danger to freedom of speech by the mass media motor mouth. There are forever among us these with an axe to grind, at lost cause to champion, a self interest to promote. The courts and the mass media seem to gravitate to such people. The power of the court has already been covered in more than one section of this document. The mass media in some ways is even more powerful. The mass media can take a tiny blip the size of a pinhead on the radar screen and with its' coverage and repetition can make that pinhead appeared to the viewer as a 747 jumbo jet coming at you from 100 yards away at 635 MPH and aimed square center on your nose. The net result is that in some areas the courts and the media would deny you the right of freedom of speech. And further the victim of a politically correct attack may also be punished for being so

frank as to exercise his right to speak out. Note this is not trial
by jury punishment. This is a mob lynching made possible by
the mass media based on pressure exerted by the parties that
wish to deny this guy freedom of speech.

Even as this is written there is an ugly scene being played out
on the television between national public radio executives and
Juan Williams. Please pay close attention readers. This episode
defines political correctness as a violation of a citizen's right of
freedom of speech. Had I personally orchestrated this event I
could not have made a more perfect example of intimidation
by political correctness. Courts where are you. You need to
speak up and be heard! Justice, justice, justice!

National Public Radio which disgracefully is funded by some
public money has for years broadcast biased programs and
gotten by with this abuse of public trust. Perhaps this time
their high-handed arrogant conduct has gone too far for even
many of the left wing. Be clear, this conduct had gone on
for many years basically without challenge. But this incident
with Williams was so violent, so obvious and so wrong that
many even of the left wing were stunned and appalled. But
for the typical Independent or Republican this is just another
day at National Public Radio only with more visibility. Let's
not rejoice too soon that some liberals have had their eyes
opened. As soon as the shock has worn off many of them will
go back to ground and the first thing you know it will all be
Juan Williams fault and NPR will be portrayed as pure as
driven snow. Remember the earlier words in this book - the
liberal will sacrifice his own mother to maintain his political
correctness stance. A big lie will not bother them in the least.

In summary the American is given freedom of speech by
the United States Constitution. There are no constitutional
restrictions. Should anyone, including a court or judge,
attempt to regulate your speech in anyway, for any purpose
that person, that judge or that court is attempting to deny
you your freedom of speech and he is the person that should
be jailed. All speech control efforts in the name of political
correctness are unconstitutional and the American citizen is

not required to comply.

6. Legislative power: Once again why debate the obvious. The United States Constitution clearly states that ALL legislative powers belong to the Congress of the United States. So where do the courts get authorization to execute decrees which in fact, are of a legislative nature. Through somewhere between boldness and insolence the courts just does it and since they have had no serious challenges it gets easier day by day. The list is endless and includes everything from school buses, to homosexuals, to prayer. The courts have involved themselves in matters of the everyday citizens such that tomorrow it may specify what each of us has for breakfast. Some of you may say ridiculous and perhaps it is - but I would not bet my life on it. Just recently a father wanted to take his little daughter to church while the ex-wife objected by filing a suit to prevent the father from taking his little daughter to church. The results of the court's actions has not been made available yet; but the mere fact that a Federal Court is even hearing such a case tells one that no eggs for breakfast could become a reality!

Briefly, the courts have found it easy to control efforts of the executive and legislative branches of the federal government to deviate from the constitution, but powerless to control its' own violation of the constitution.

In summary, courts that issue pronouncements that are legislative in nature are an invasion of congressional responsibility and authority as defined in the United States constitution and therefore null and void. Any such decree is therefore not to be honored by the American citizen or by the governmental or private agencies.

To summarize the summaries: The Supreme Court routinely violates its oath of office therefore its oath is not worth a pinch of salt. Please read the sentence again slowly and allow the gigantic significance of that to seep deep into your heart and mind.

To be fair to the court allow me to draw the reader's attention to these areas of the constitution where the court "interprets" something – but does not <u>violate</u> a clearly written statement. I make a distinction. In these decisions where 1) there is no violation of the words in the constitution, 2) where the decision is supported by a majority of the citizens and 3) where the decision is just I believe these to stand on their own merits. And the proper way to ensure that is called an amendment. In the six areas just reviewed; however the court is violating the constitution and the citizens are no more required to honor their decisions then they are a decision telling them to go jump in the lake. Every time the court violates the clear words of the constitution it is saying, in effect, "I may have lied to get here, but I'm here now and there is not a damn thing you can do about it!"

AND THE COW JUMPED OVER THE MOON

During a soccer game one of my little granddaughters was asked to explain something she said to one of the other teams players. Now readers, read this close for I want you to fully understand what happens when the courts stray from the constitution and go through their "interpretation" routine. This is the ultimate trickledown effect of endless interpretations of the prior interpretations. The constitution reads "...no law respecting an establishment of religion or prohibiting the free exercise thereof..." the courts strayed from this clear passage to a fantasy of "...separation of church and state...".

And now back to my granddaughter and her soccer game. Her coach called her aside and asked if she said something like "you need to go to church" to one of the girls on the opposing team. My granddaughter said "Yes, I did." Her coach asked why she said it. My granddaughters' response was: "Well, it was the nicest thing I could think of to say when she called me a butt-sniffer."

Apparently, not anticipating that my granddaughter would take offense at being called a "butt-sniffer" the other girl had been so indoctrinated in political correctness even at her young age that she knew she was supposed to be offended at anything coming within a mile of "religion" that she reported my granddaughters comment to her coach. Her coach being equally indoctrinated instead of telling the child to "get over it", walked across the field and said something to my granddaughters coach. Her coach being equally indoctrinated instead of telling the other coach to get "get over it" said something to my sweet and lovely granddaughter. I am proud of my granddaughter for her self-control; however had it been me at that age the offending opponent would not have gotten off so lightly and that is a true story.

Of course, the engine that drives this madness is the courts. The courts make it possible while the mass media provides the fire power to kill any sane conduct and promote insane conduct. The evils of political correctness and the trashing of the constitution by such absurdities as "separation of church and state" are directly responsible for this outrageous and ugly scene at a little girls soccer game in Mississippi – far from the court in Washington and the media motor mouths in New York.

In their deliberations on some issue the court is either incapable of seeing the ripple effect of their decisions or they could not care less about the ripple effect. After all it is only the entire population the United States minus 9 judges that have to deal with the problem(s) they create. In some degree, each decision restricts our freedom of action and/or speech.

Incidentally, under the constitution as written although what the girl said to my granddaughter was and is a lie she had the right to say it and that what my granddaughter said in response she had the right to say and I believe her response to be the truth.

The American people should not only reject political correctness, but should fight tooth and nail. They should also work with equal vigor to remove judges violating their oath of office, i.e. violating the constitution.

Now, if the Supreme Court wants to change the constitution; that is okay. There is an established and legal procedure to do that. It's called an amendment and if the court wants to change the constitution they must do it as all others must do--the long and difficult process of the amendment.

I accuse the United States Supreme Court:

1. Of violating the oath of office taken by every court member

2. Of violating the United States Constitution in countless ways and for countless times

3. Of illegally amending the constitution by distorting the clearly written word of the constitution to suit their own purposes and agenda.

4. Of denying the right of the majority to live as they wish; to decide the present and the future of the country by giving a single individual the power to set the agenda for the entire country and to have his way at the expense of the majority.

5. Of turning its' ear, its' eye and its' head to more countless violations of the United States Constitution by lower courts.

Intimidation by political correctness is but one of the many examples of failure to uphold the constitution of which I accuse the United States Supreme Court. The court apparently does not understand or does not care that in granting one individual his hearts' desire, it is denying the hearts' desire of millions of other citizens. Nor is it awake to the fact that there has been and always will be a person or group of people that are unhappy with the circumstances of life. I am very, very unhappy with the status of the United States of America at this very moment but I do not think for even one microsecond that the Supreme Court if going to do anything about it because my desires would not fit their SOCIAL PICTURE BOOK.